THE
IOWA
CAUCUS

THE
IOWA
CAUCUS

RACHEL PAINE CAUFIELD

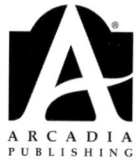

ARCADIA
PUBLISHING

Published by Arcadia Publishing
Charleston, South Carolina

Printed in the United States of America

Library of Congress Control Number: 2015956912

For all general information, please contact Arcadia Publishing:
Telephone 843-853-2070
Fax 843-853-0044
E-mail sales@arcadiapublishing.com
For customer service and orders:
Toll-Free 1-888-313-2665

Visit us on the Internet at www.arcadiapublishing.com

Dedicated to the people of Iowa and the activists that make the caucuses possible. Watching them engage with the process restores one's faith in the political system.

CONTENTS

Acknowledgments   6

Introduction   7

1.   Retail Politics Is Real   9

2.   Meeting and Greeting Large and Small   27

3.   Rituals and Customs New and Old   47

4.   Media Is Here, There, and Everywhere   63

5.   All Eyes on Iowa   79

ACKNOWLEDGMENTS

When one first encounters the Iowa caucus, it is like falling down the rabbit hole of American politics—disorienting and thrilling. It feels unreal. Where else can average voters shake hands with multiple presidential candidates in a single evening? Where else do our nation's highest officeholders stroll down the street aiming to meet locals? Where else do we gather with friends, family, and neighbors on a snowy night to have civil discussion of issues and know that our voices will shape the course of history? The political environment that has grown up around the Iowa caucuses is very special.

Every day, I have the pleasure of working with people who care deeply about politics: students, colleagues, and friends. Since arriving in Iowa, they have each played a vital role in my own caucus experiences. Dennis Goldford and Arthur Sanders have been outstanding mentors in caucus land, along with colleagues Debra DeLaet and Joanna Mosser, who have indulged my preoccupation with the caucuses through four presidential campaign cycles.

I am also thankful for the excellent staff at the Harkin Institute for Public Policy and Citizen Engagement, who are building a legacy of research and outreach for the next generation of leaders in Iowa and around the nation, including Marsha Ternus, Estelle Montgomery, Amy Beller, and David Redlawsk, along with the Iowa Caucus Project team. The new Harkin Collection at Drake University's Archives and Special Collections and political papers archivist Hope Grebner were instrumental in creating this book and a repository of knowledge for all citizens.

In compiling this book, I am indebted to the individuals who graciously shared images and experiences. Des Moines native Jordan Oster is a tireless documentarian of the campaign events he attends. Keith Wessel has shared beautiful photographs from his years on the campaign trail. The staff of the State Historical Society of Iowa and the University of Iowa Special Collections were very helpful, as was the staff of the Republican Party of Iowa.

Together, their photographs tell the story of the Iowa caucuses. It has been my privilege to work with all of them to share the story.

INTRODUCTION

It is an overcast March morning in Des Moines. The 2016 presidential election is just shy of 20 months away. Nearly 1,000 people, plus 250 reporters, are convening at the Iowa State Fairgrounds to see the Republican presidential candidates at the Iowa Ag Summit, the brainchild of activist Bruce Rastetter. One by one, candidates take the stage to answer questions about energy, ethanol, the environment, and myriad other issues. At the back of the room, reporters swarm to get a photograph of each contender as they enter the building. It is safe to assume that most of the people in the room are here because they want a first glimpse of the many contenders who will spend the year in Iowa competing for the presidency: Mike Huckabee, Ted Cruz, Scott Walker, Jeb Bush, Lindsey Graham, Chris Christie, Rick Perry, George Pataki, and Rick Santorum.

Events like the Iowa Ag Summit provide unparalleled access to the nation's leaders, and Iowa voters have what can only be described as an exceptional role to play in determining who will become the next president. Though they almost certainly did not consider it at the time, those who attended the Iowa Ag Summit were part of a well-established and unique experience on the road to the White House. The Iowa caucuses have created a vibrant political atmosphere unlike any other in the world, with the possible exception of New Hampshire, which has held the first-in-the-nation primary since 1918. And voters are the heart and soul of that process.

Iowa has always had a caucus, which is best described as a system in which party leaders convene for in-person meetings to define the party's platform, choose the party's candidates, and elect party officers. It was not until 1972 that Iowa's caucuses became part of the fabric of the national nomination campaign. The tumultuous 1968 Democratic Convention in Chicago exposed deep divisions within the party, and then-chairman of the Democratic National Committee Fred Harris appointed a commission to address the problems. That commission, chaired by George McGovern and Donald Fraser, recommended a set of policy changes to make the party's nomination procedures more transparent and inclusive. Among the recommendations was a rule that delegates to the national party convention would be chosen in a way that allowed open participation at the local level. Thus, any state holding a caucus would need to reform their system to include local party meetings rather than one statewide party meeting, a change intended to distribute more power to citizen activists and rank-and-file voters. After Democratic state legislators passed legal and regulatory reforms, a number of rule changes, including this one, would subsequently be applied to the Republican Party as well.

Meanwhile, the Iowa Democratic Party was ahead of the curve and had already crafted a system of local caucuses. The state party set up a four-stage process allowing all party voters to participate in small-scale local meetings (precinct caucuses) and elect delegates to county conventions. At the county convention, party voters would elect delegates for a convention representing all counties in a congressional district. At the district convention, party voters would elect delegates to a statewide convention, at which delegates to the national convention would be selected. Each stage required a good deal of logistical organization, and those constructing the plan built in time to print and distribute information, such as proposed planks to the party platform, to the delegates. Working backward from the date of the national convention, the date of the precinct caucuses had to be early. Because it used a caucus rather than a primary, Iowa was permitted to move its date ahead of the New Hampshire contest.

And so it was that in 1972, as political leaders anxiously watched a new system of rules go into effect, Iowa held the first contest to select party nominees for the presidency. Little attention was paid to the affair; President Nixon was unchallenged in his reelection bid, and only two Democrats, George McGovern and Edmund Muskie, competed for the Democratic nomination (Muskie tied with those voting "uncommitted," which was deemed a loss because he did not meet expectations; McGovern went on to win the nomination but lose the presidency).

It was a little-known Southern governor, Jimmy Carter, who put the Iowa caucuses on the map. Carter had neither the money nor the name recognition to launch a viable national campaign for the presidency in 1976. To remedy these deficiencies, he opted to focus on Iowa as a springboard, hoping to outperform other candidates and draw media attention to his campaign. Carter campaigned heavily in the state, using one-on-one meetings so that voters could get to know him. His investment paid off, propelling him to the presidency. Though uncommitted again won more votes in the caucus than any candidate, Carter vastly exceeded expectations by drawing the support of 27 percent, more than double that of any other named candidate. Since 1976, candidates in both parties have emulated Carter's strategy of campaigning early and often in the state.

Today, the Iowa caucuses draw national and international media attention, and candidates lavish attention on the state to build strong grassroots organizations and turn out caucus-goers. A win—or even a stronger-than-expected showing—can bring a big bump in name recognition and fundraising for the coming contests across the country. Most campaigns invest heavily in their Iowa campaign, though it remains a place where investments of time and energy are typically more valuable than television advertising. Iowa voters expect the same person-to-person campaigning that characterized early races before the 24-hour news cycle or the rise of robocalls.

Although the caucuses have been garnering attention for 40 years, the ebb and flow of the electoral environment defines the level of competition. During the 1980s, for example, Republicans had incumbent presidents in 1980 and 1984. Iowa senator Tom Harkin's 1992 bid discouraged other contenders from launching campaigns in the state, and a Republican incumbent (George H.W. Bush) was unchallenged during that cycle. In 1988 and 2000, sitting vice presidents were seeking the presidency, though the opposing party witnessed a competitive field in both cycles. Since 1972, only two cycles have featured open contests in both parties, with no incumbent president or vice president in the race: 2008 and 2016.

In their infancy, the Iowa caucuses were modest events. Candidates visited the state, met with voters, and hoped that their efforts would pay off. Four decades later, candidates still visit the state, meet with voters, and hope that their efforts will yield results. But the caucus system has matured over time. The bright lights of media cameras have become commonplace, traditions have been established, and those seeking to shape the national issue agenda have found their way to Iowa. Amid these changes, those who have the privilege of witnessing it often come away from the experience knowing that there is something special that happens here. In an age of cynicism, when many Americans feel disconnected from the political process, the Iowa caucuses feature something rare and beautiful—real people who care about real issues directly engaging with the nation's political leaders. For those of us who have the good fortune to participate, the Iowa caucuses are the essence of participatory democracy.

One

Retail Politics is Real

Iowa is known for "retail politics," a process in which candidates engage with voters face to face and person to person. Unlike most states, Iowa features intimate gatherings, direct interactions, and awkward moments as the candidates meet with voters, take questions, and introduce themselves to the citizens who will determine their fate. Over the course of many months, the campaigns directly engage voters, and many voters test the waters by taking the opportunity to see multiple candidates multiple times. It may surprise many non-Iowans to learn that more than 1,600 precinct caucuses take place across the state for each party on caucus night. With more than 3,000 party meetings taking place in a state with approximately three million people, the first thing to know is that the process is intensely local. Some caucuses have hundreds of attendees, while others will have a handful of people joining together in someone's living room, a public library, or the local elementary school. At each one of those caucuses, community members will stand up to speak on behalf of each campaign, which elevates the citizen activist to a particularly important role in Iowa. Every campaign seeks to find more than 1,600 dedicated volunteers to articulate the candidate's message and serve as an effective advocate. To be a viable contender in the Iowa caucuses, a candidate must connect directly with average voters in the hopes of attracting a strong grassroots base of supporters who can propel the campaign to victory on caucus night. Doing so requires a substantial commitment of time shaking hands and answering questions, seeking any opportunity to speak directly to voters.

Some have characterized this process as being peculiar and parochial (at best) or undemocratic (at worst). Some argue that the state's agricultural interests and predominantly white population make it a poor choice to perform such an important function, as it does not accurately reflect the makeup of the country. And some say that the rules and procedures that govern the caucuses, particularly for the Democratic Party, are outdated, arcane, or confusing. Nonetheless, and despite continual calls to change the process, Iowa continues to maintain its first-in-the-nation status. One justification for allowing Iowa to lead the party-nomination process is that retail politics permits all candidates to compete on a level playing field. The Iowa caucuses are not about name recognition and campaign spending. Here, candidates succeed by meeting real people, listening to real concerns, and answering real questions.

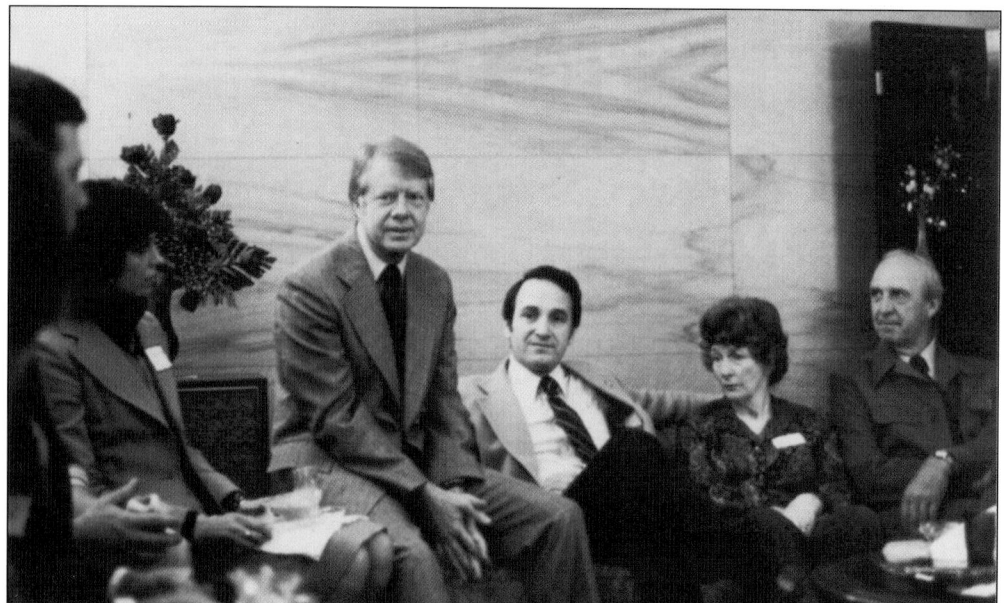

Jimmy Carter's 1976 campaign for the presidency was a turning point for Iowa. Though Iowa had been first in the nation in 1972, Carter invested significant time in small-group campaigning, believing that a come-from-behind win in Iowa could provide the momentum to elevate his viability nationally. He beat all other candidates, and his tactics have become the model for all subsequent campaigns. (Courtesy of the Harkin Collection, Drake University Archives and Special Collections.)

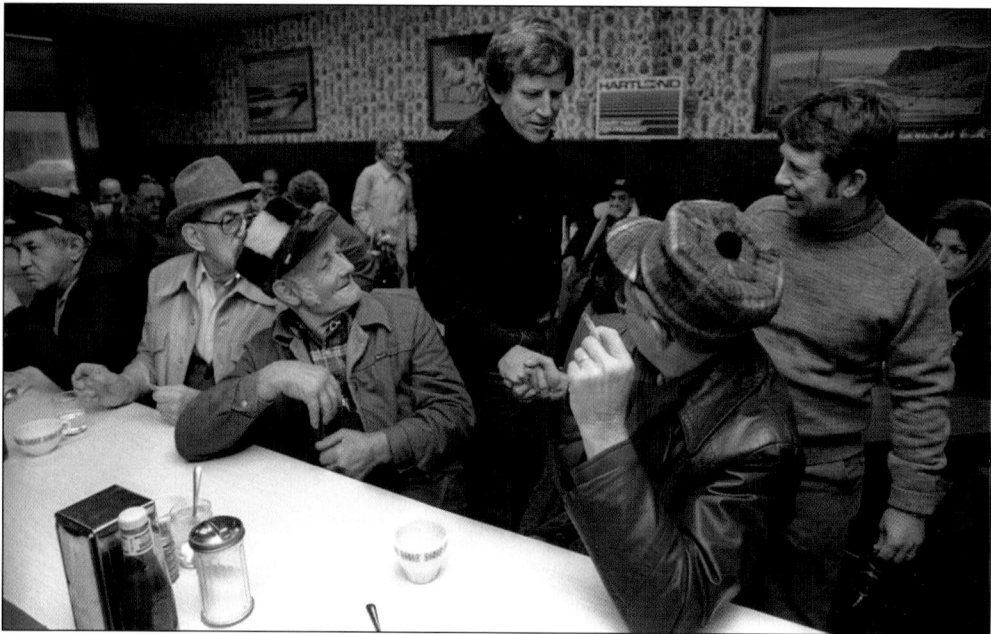

Retail politics require a good deal of time and energy. Candidates are found shaking hands and meeting voters in small-town restaurants, VFW halls, and high school gymnasiums across the state. Here, presidential candidate Gary Hart meets and greets voters in a small-town diner. (Courtesy of Keith Wessel.)

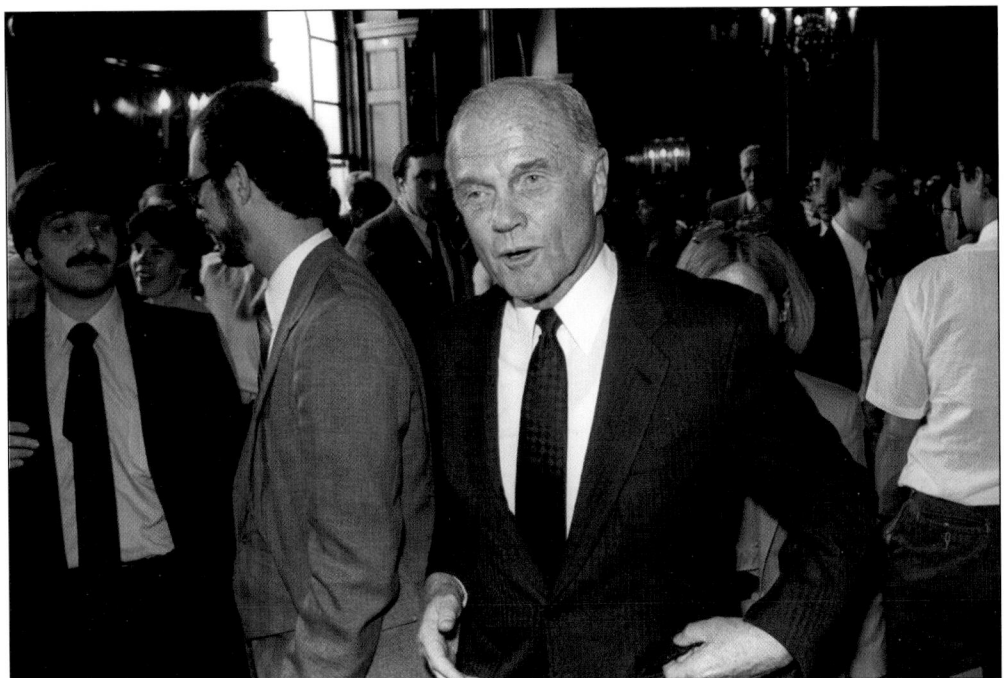

John Glenn was an early favorite for the Democratic nomination in 1983. According to the *New York Times*: "Babies are thrust at him. He is asked to autograph $20 bills or shirt cuffs or, at a country airport in Iowa, the cover of a 1962 issue of *Life* magazine that bears his photograph over the worshipful caption 'The Making of a Brave Man.' " He was briefly running a tight second to Walter Mondale in a fall poll but ended the caucuses with only four percent support. Glenn is pictured here attending a meet and greet in Iowa. (Courtesy of Keith Wessel.)

Although the media allows a national audience to watch candidates as they come through Iowa during the final months before the caucuses, would-be candidates frequently come to the state to meet activists and raise their profile in the state long before the media tunes in to the race. Here, Mark Warner speaks after the 2005 Harkin Steak Fry in an Indianola bar. (Courtesy of Jordan Oster.)

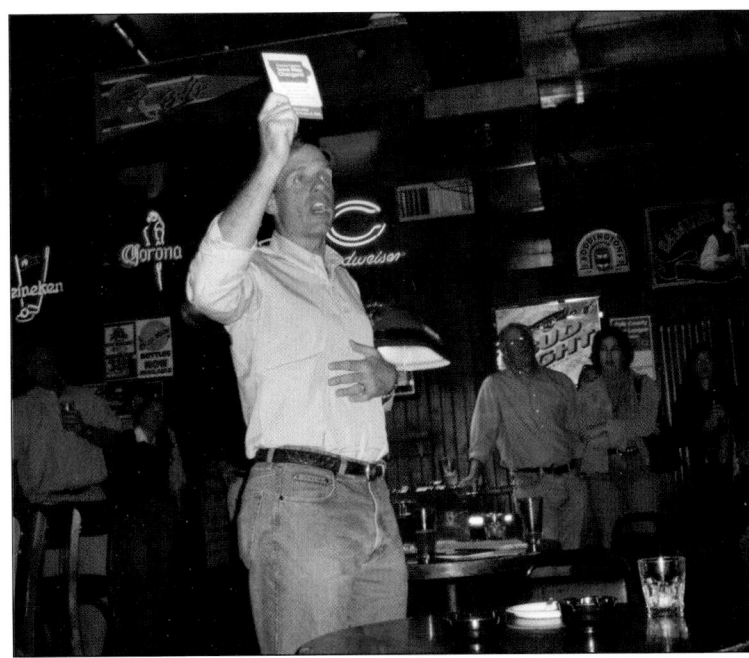

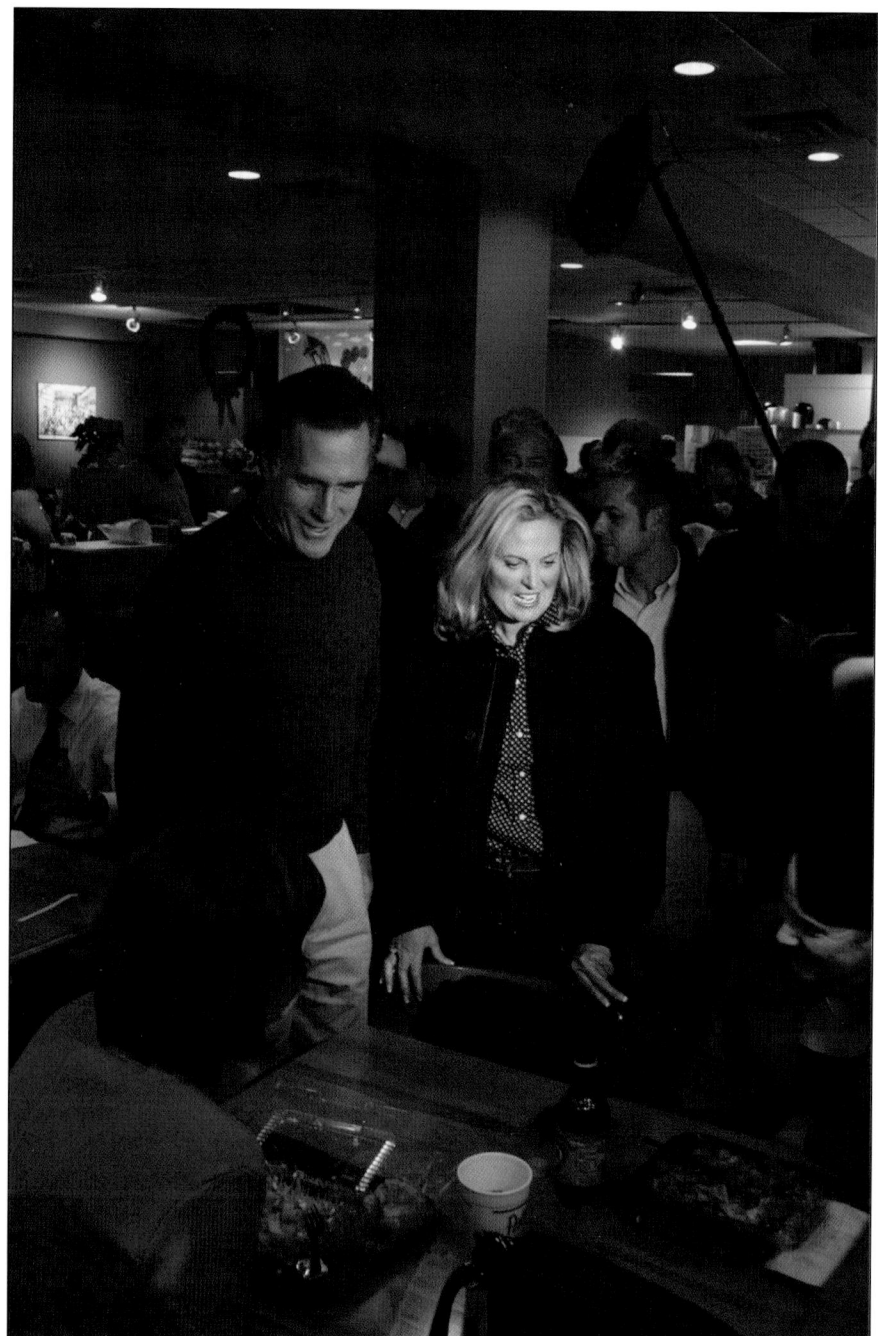

Local restaurants often host presidential candidates who stop by to shake hands and introduce themselves to voters. Diners are so frequently interrupted by candidates and journalists that one company printed special T-shirts for visiting journalists in 2015, one of which reads, "Sorry to interrupt your meal, but are you alive and have an opinion on the upcoming election?" Mitt Romney, pictured here at a West Des Moines restaurant with his wife, Ann, was bested twice in the Iowa caucus (by Mike Huckabee in 2008 and by Rick Santorum in 2012) but became the Republican nominee in 2012. (Courtesy of Jordan Oster.)

Meeting with Iowa voters frequently includes stops at local restaurants, as when former Wisconsin governor Tommy Thompson met with voters over pizza at The Tavern in West Des Moines. Thompson was in the race for just four months, dropping out after a disappointing sixth-place finish in the Republican Party of Iowa Straw Poll in August 2007. (Courtesy of Jordan Oster.)

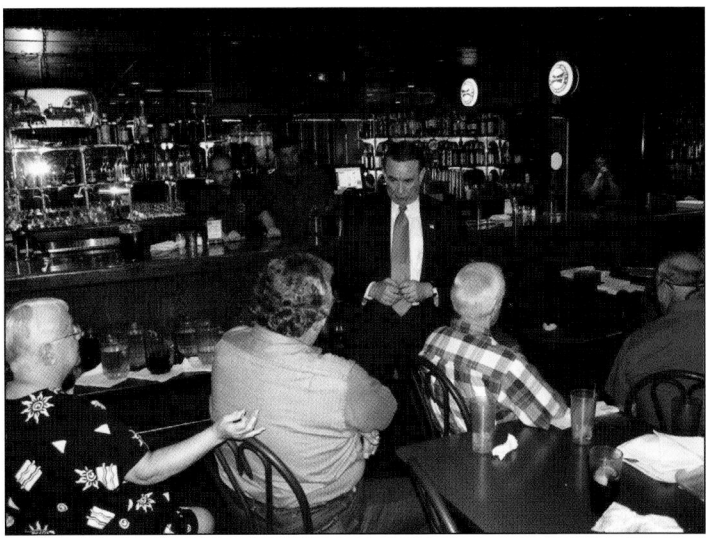

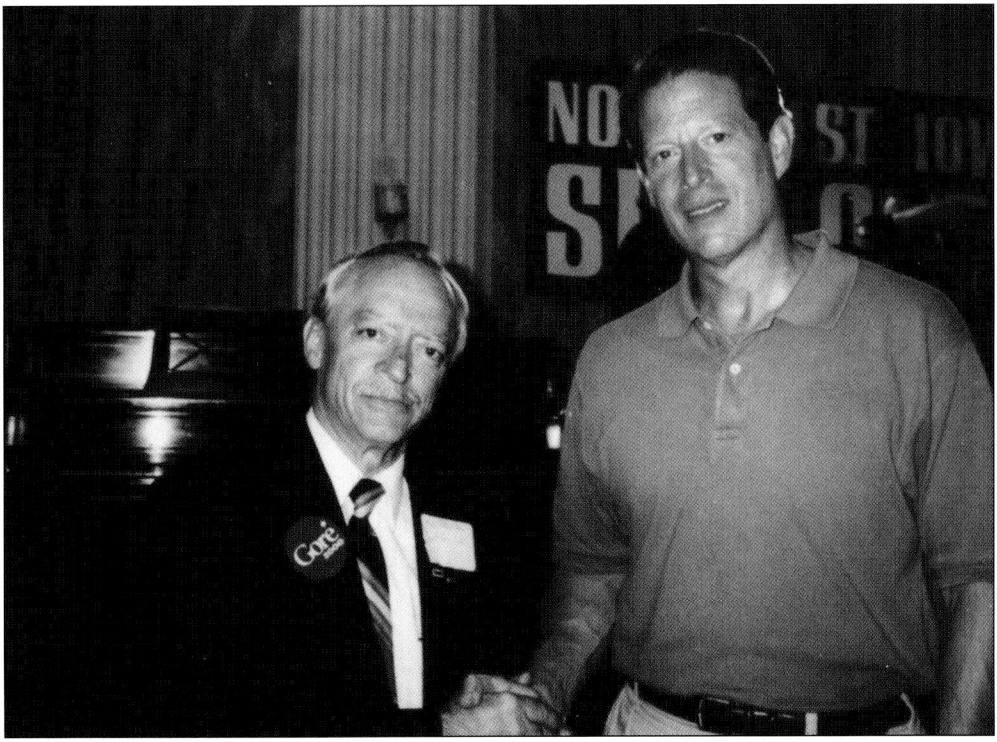

The hallmark of the Iowa caucuses is the regular one-on-one meetings between candidates and voters. A frequent joke references the fact that most Iowa voters cannot make up their mind even after meeting a candidate five or six times. Al Gore is pictured here meeting with a supporter in northwest Iowa at a meeting of labor unions in 1999. (Courtesy of the Harkin Collection, Drake University Archives and Special Collections.)

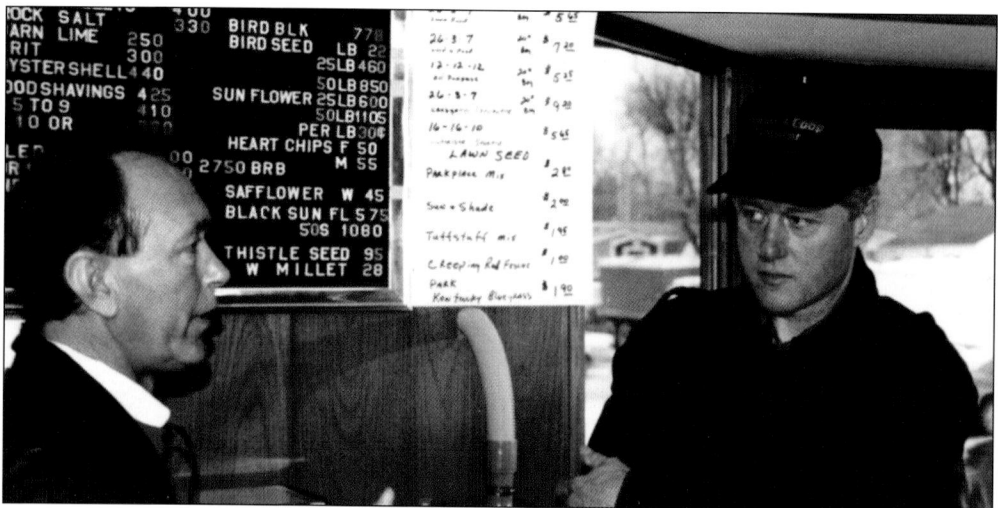

To introduce themselves to Iowa voters and community leaders, candidates frequently visit local businesses for closed events with managers and employees. Bill Clinton, former governor of Arkansas, meets a voter at a feed store. With Iowa senator Tom Harkin in the race in 1992, Clinton did not mount a significant campaign, but he returned prior to his 1996 reelection effort. (Courtesy of the Harkin Collection, Drake University Archives and Special Collections.)

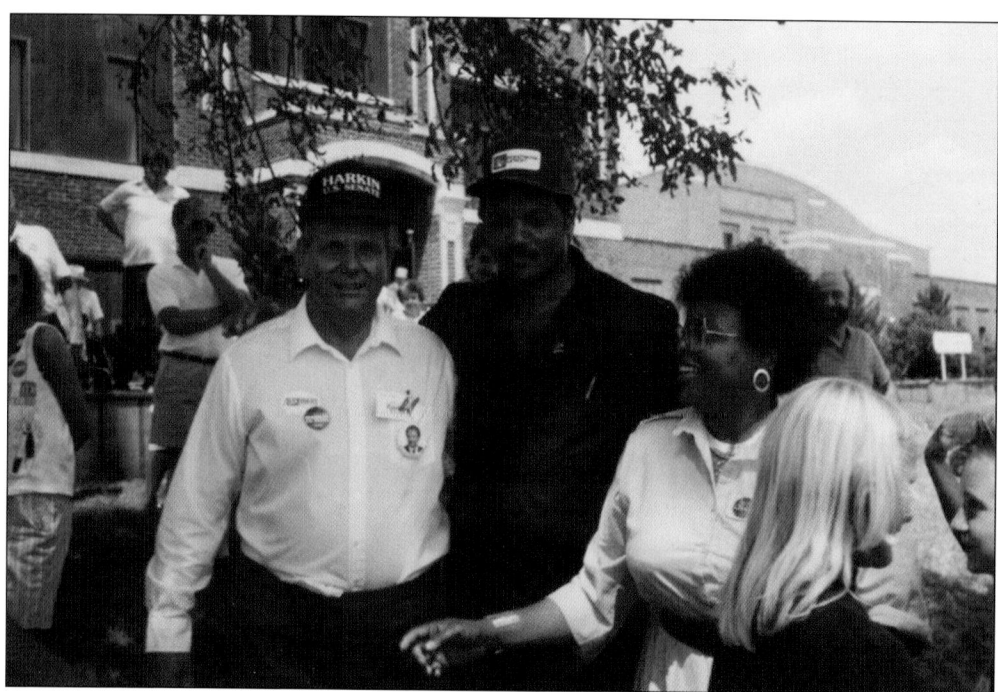

Ralph Johnson of Bloomfield, Iowa, is pictured here with Jesse Jackson during a visit in 1990 in Davis County. After an unsuccessful run in 1984, Jackson's 1988 campaign was considered to be much more organized. After losing again in 1988, Jackson continued to come to Iowa, and some anticipated that he might launch another bid in 1992. (Courtesy of the Harkin Collection, Drake University Archives and Special Collections.)

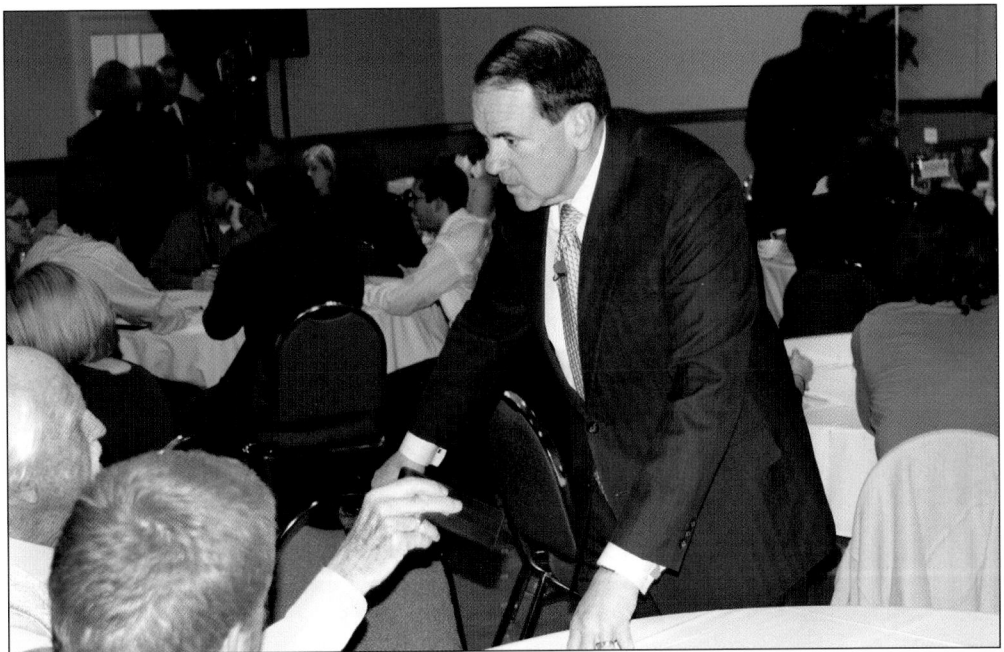

Former governor of Arkansas Mike Huckabee entered the race for the Republican nomination on January 28, 2007. His folksy style, Christian conservatism, and campaign concerts (Huckabee plays bass) made him popular on the campaign trail. He went on to win the 2008 Iowa caucuses with 34 percent of the vote despite spending far less than other candidates. (Courtesy of Jordan Oster.)

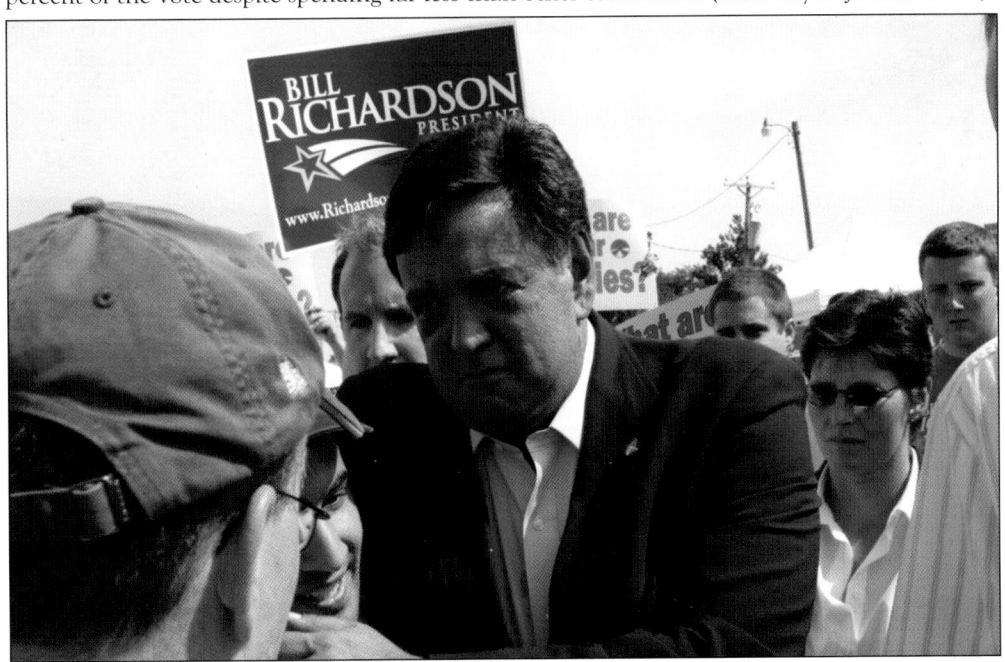

Former governor of New Mexico Bill Richardson meets with Iowa voters at an outdoor rally. Richardson was the first major candidate of Hispanic descent. He withdrew from the race one week after the 2008 Iowa caucus following fourth-place finishes in both Iowa and New Hampshire. (Courtesy of Jordan Oster.)

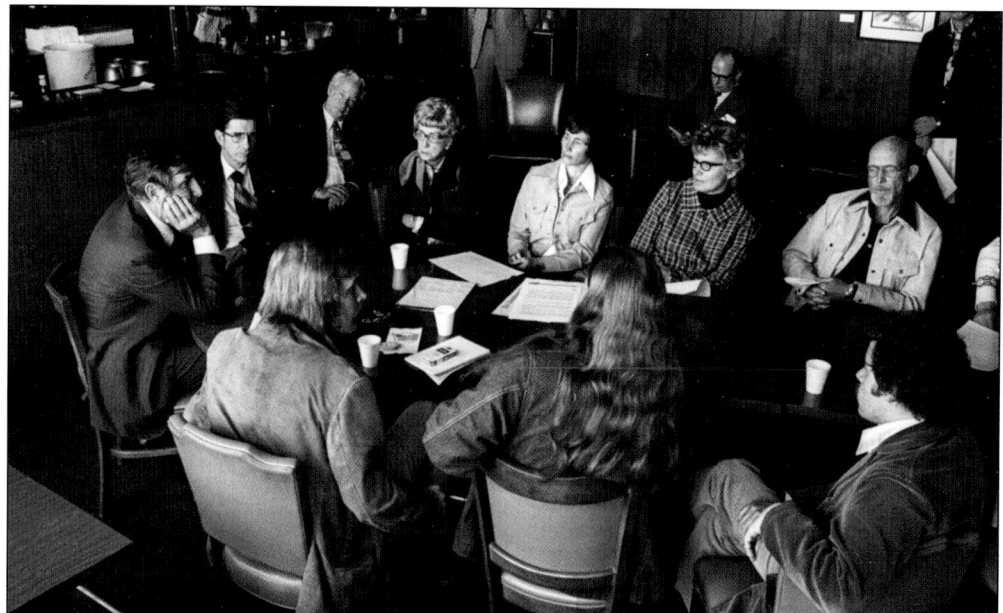

Rep. Morris K. "Mo" Udall (D-AZ) meets with activists and staff members in 1974, more than 16 months ahead of the 1976 Iowa caucuses. After new rules had gone into effect in 1972, Democrats saw an opportunity to use the first-in-the-nation caucuses to generate momentum for their campaign. This is exactly the tactic used by Udall's rival Jimmy Carter, who went on to win second place behind uncommitted. Udall, meanwhile, came in fifth. (Courtesy of Keith Wessel.)

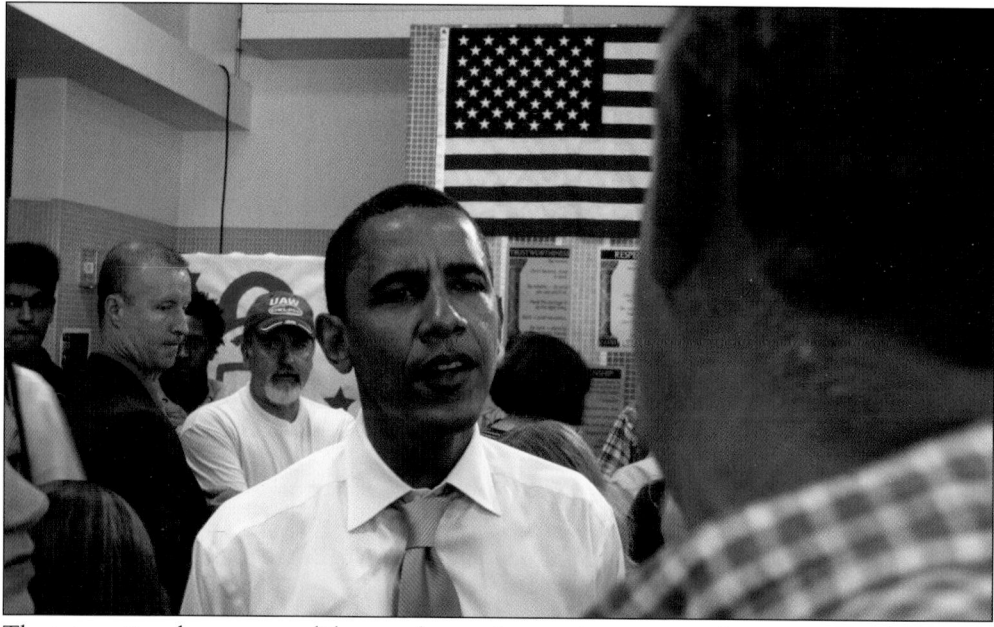

The interactions between candidates and voters happen in a variety of settings across the state of Iowa. Although Sen. Hillary Clinton was widely accepted as the likely Democratic nominee in 2008, Sen. Barack Obama's extensive voter outreach efforts (including this meeting in Newton, Iowa) in the year leading up to the caucuses yielded a big win on caucus night, with Clinton coming in third. (Courtesy of Jordan Oster.)

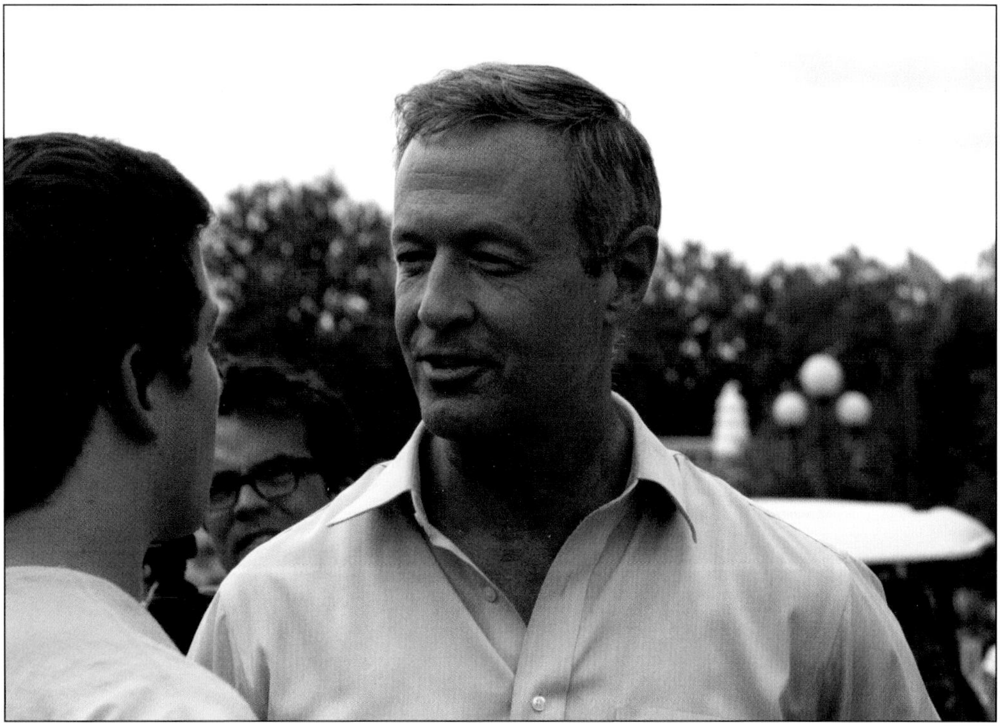

Even at large-scale events like the Iowa State Fair, candidates take any opportunity to speak with individual voters one on one. Politically minded Iowa voters have a chance to ask questions in a variety of settings, as this fairgoer did when he encountered Martin O'Malley after the candidate visited the *Des Moines Register* Soapbox in 2015. (Author's collection.)

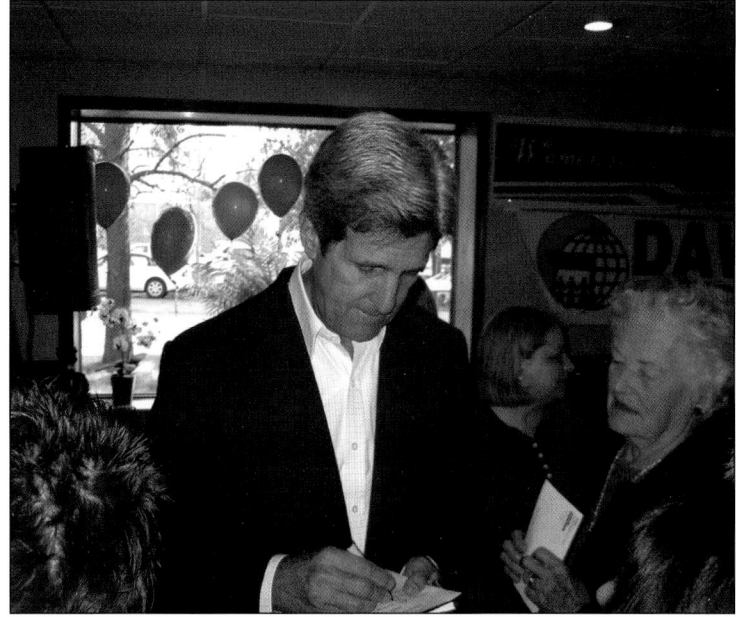

John Kerry won the 2004 Iowa caucus with strong support from labor unions across the state. Just months after losing the presidency to George W. Bush, Kerry returned to Iowa to attend a Democratic Women's campaign event and was widely anticipated to return to the campaign trail in the hopes of repeating his success. He ultimately decided not to run. (Courtesy of Jordan Oster.)

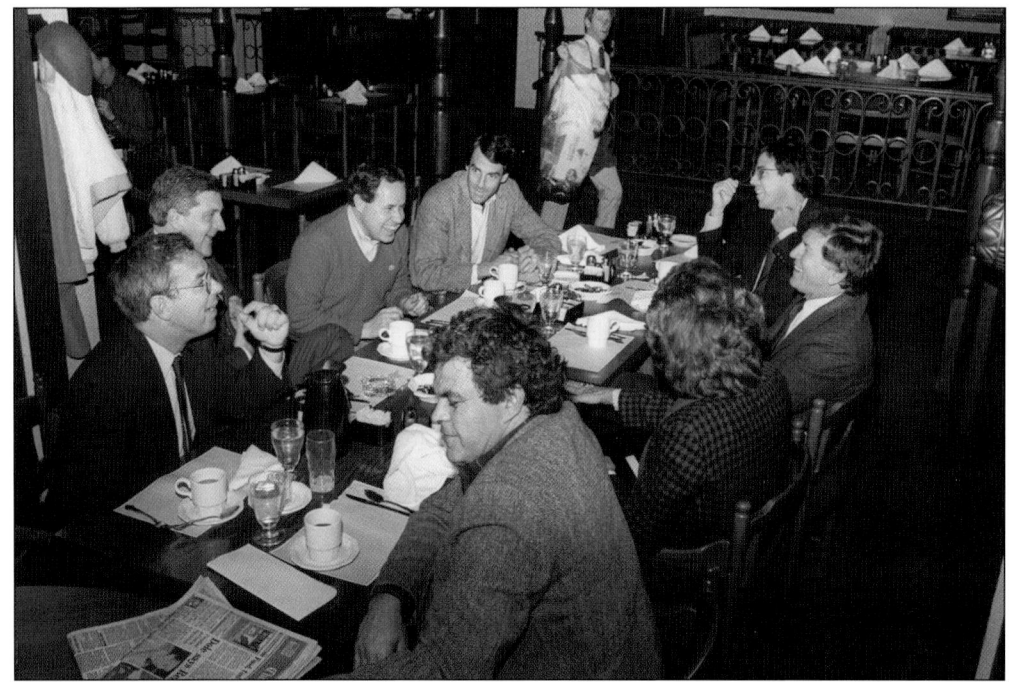

On caucus night, over 1,600 precinct caucuses are held across the state of Iowa. Campaigns know that local activists are essential supporters and often join small gatherings of Iowa voters in the hopes of attracting leaders to their campaign. Gary Hart (pictured here at a small group dinner with staff and supporters in 1987) had an extensive outreach to activists in the 1984 and 1988 campaign. He suspended his 1988 campaign after an affair was revealed. (Courtesy of Keith Wessel.)

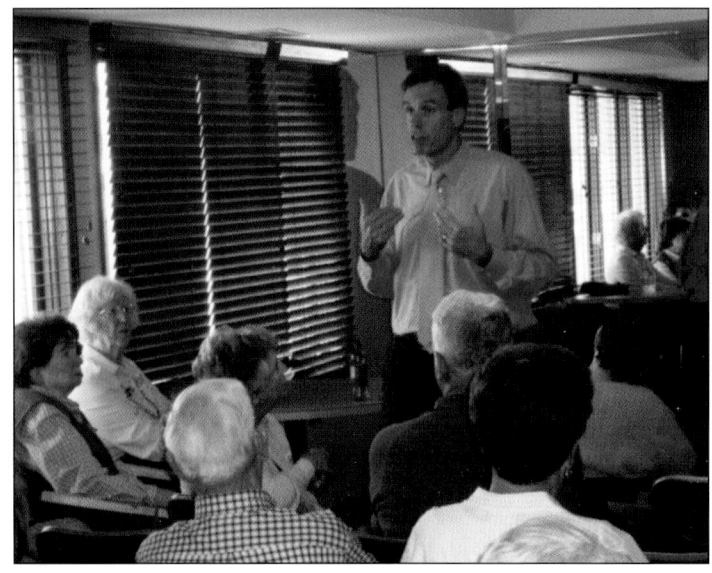

Sen. Mark Warner (D-VA) was widely considered a strong contender for the 2008 Democratic nomination and visited the state regularly in the years leading up to the race. Warner is pictured here in 2006 at an event to support Michael Mauro, a Democratic candidate for secretary of state. Warner never did declare his candidacy for the presidency. (Courtesy of Jordan Oster.)

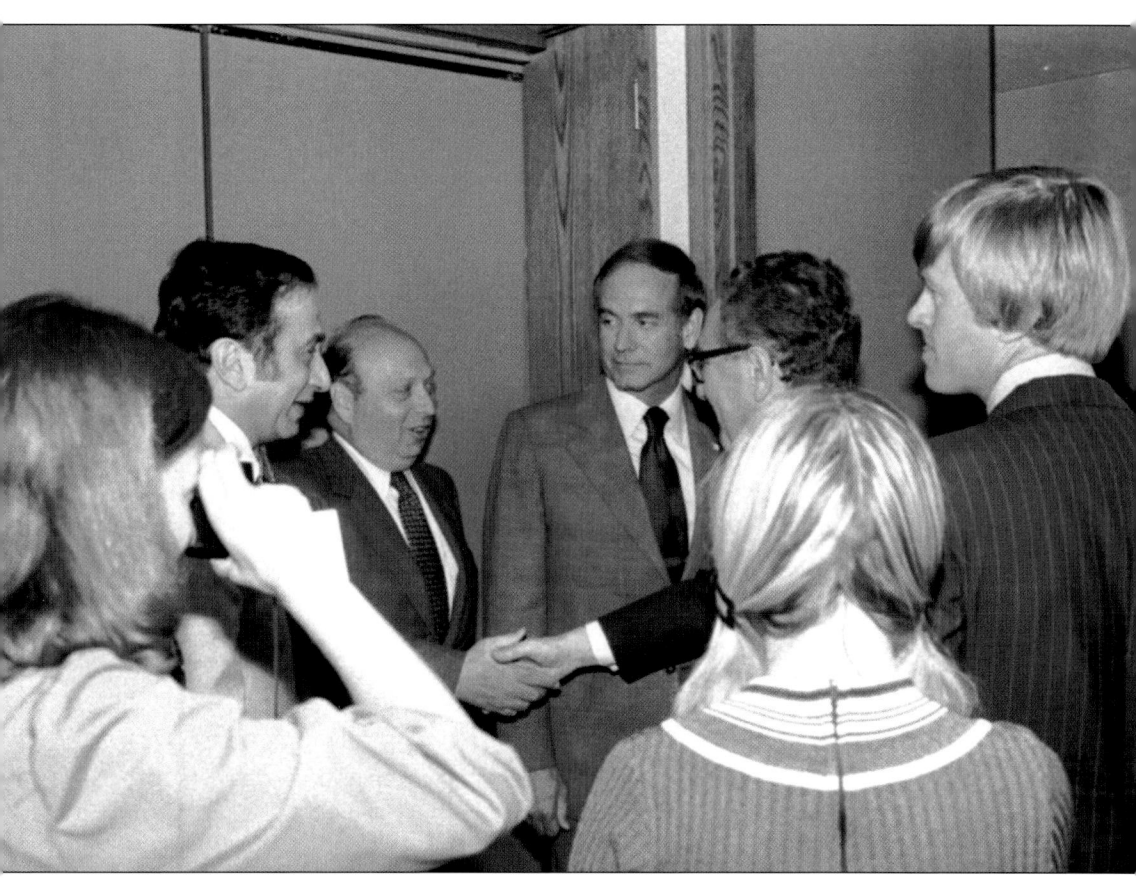

Retail politics is not only for candidates. Party leaders, elected officials, and activists frequently come to Iowa to discuss issues and meet with Iowa voters. They may come to the state to appear in support of a candidate (as a campaign surrogate), or they may simply want to maintain their Iowa connections for the future. Henry Kissinger, pictured here at a campaign event on May 22, 1979, was an outspoken critic of the Carter administration on foreign policy. He endorsed California governor Ronald Reagan as an "essentially prudent man," a move that many suggest was vital to Reagan's win over George H.W. Bush in 1980. (Courtesy of the David Penney Collection, State Historical Society of Iowa, Des Moines.)

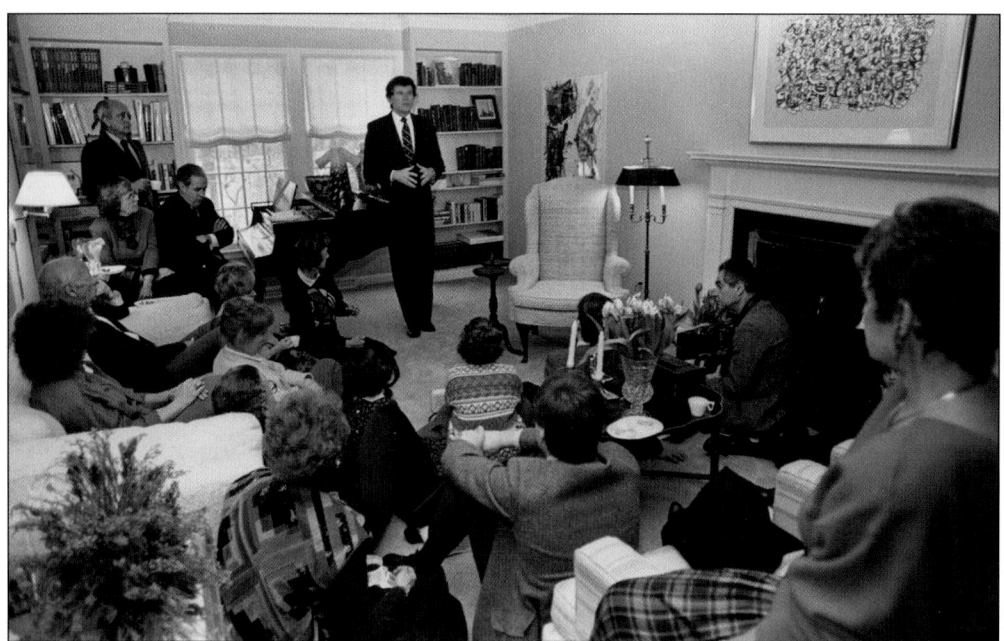

Sen. Gary Hart (D-CO) talks with activists and party supporters at the home of Elliott Erwitt. After a strong showing in the 1984 nomination campaign, Hart ran a second time in 1988. In April 1987, allegations that he was having an affair surfaced. Eventually, it was confirmed that he was having an affair with Donna Rice, which doomed his run for the presidency. (Courtesy of Keith Wessel.)

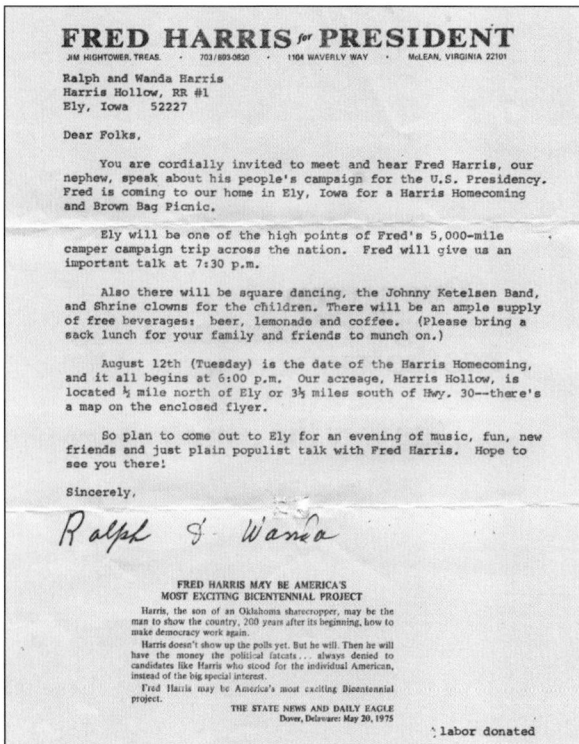

With incumbent Gerald Ford in office, all eyes were on the Democratic race in 1976. Fred Harris, former chair of the DNC who had appointed the McGovern-Fraser commission to alter the procedures to select a party nominee, launched a campaign for the presidency. Like Jimmy Carter, he focused on small events and one-on-one interactions. Here, members of his family invite neighbors to attend a brown-bag picnic with free beer as part of Harris's campaign camper tour across the country. With no money, Harris is remembered for spending nights in supporters' homes in Iowa. (Courtesy of Frank Nye Papers, University of Iowa Libraries, Iowa City, Iowa.)

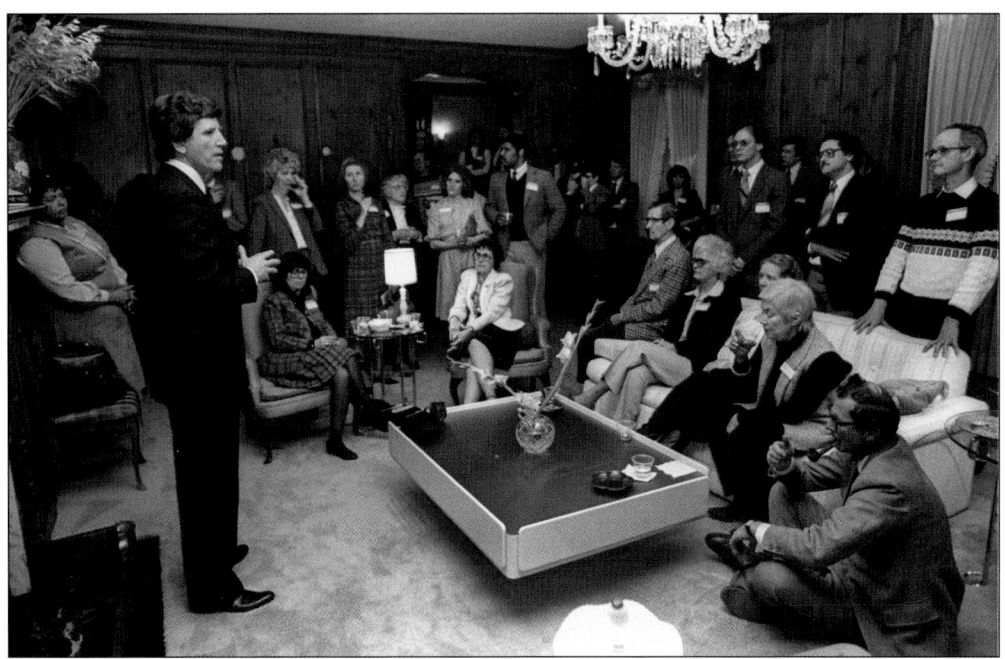

One staple of the Iowa campaign trail is the house party, in which the candidate will meet supporters in someone's home. Gary Hart, pictured above, was perceived to be a long-shot candidate against Vice Pres. Walter Mondale in 1984, but he put significant time into building relationships with voters. Though Mondale won the Iowa caucus, Hart became a formidable opponent after winning New Hampshire. Howard Baker (R-TN) is pictured below with supporters at a home following the 1979 Republican Party Lincoln Dinner. Baker polled very well, but after losing to George H.W. Bush in the Iowa caucuses and Ronald Reagan in the New Hampshire primary, he withdrew from the race. (Above, courtesy of the Harkin Collection, Drake University Archives and Special Collections; below, the State Historical Society of Iowa, Des Moines, David Penney Collection.)

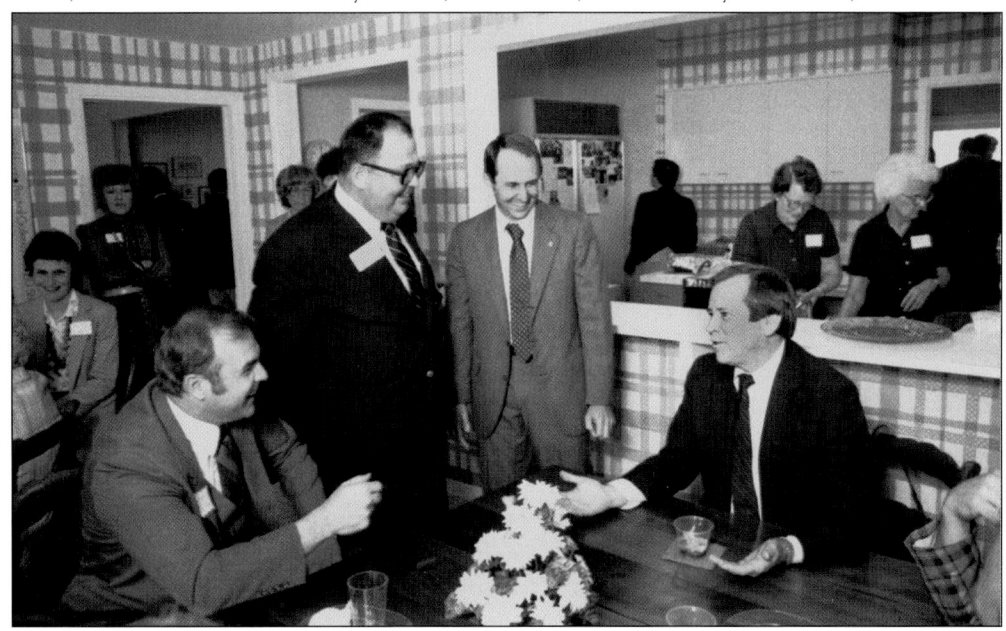

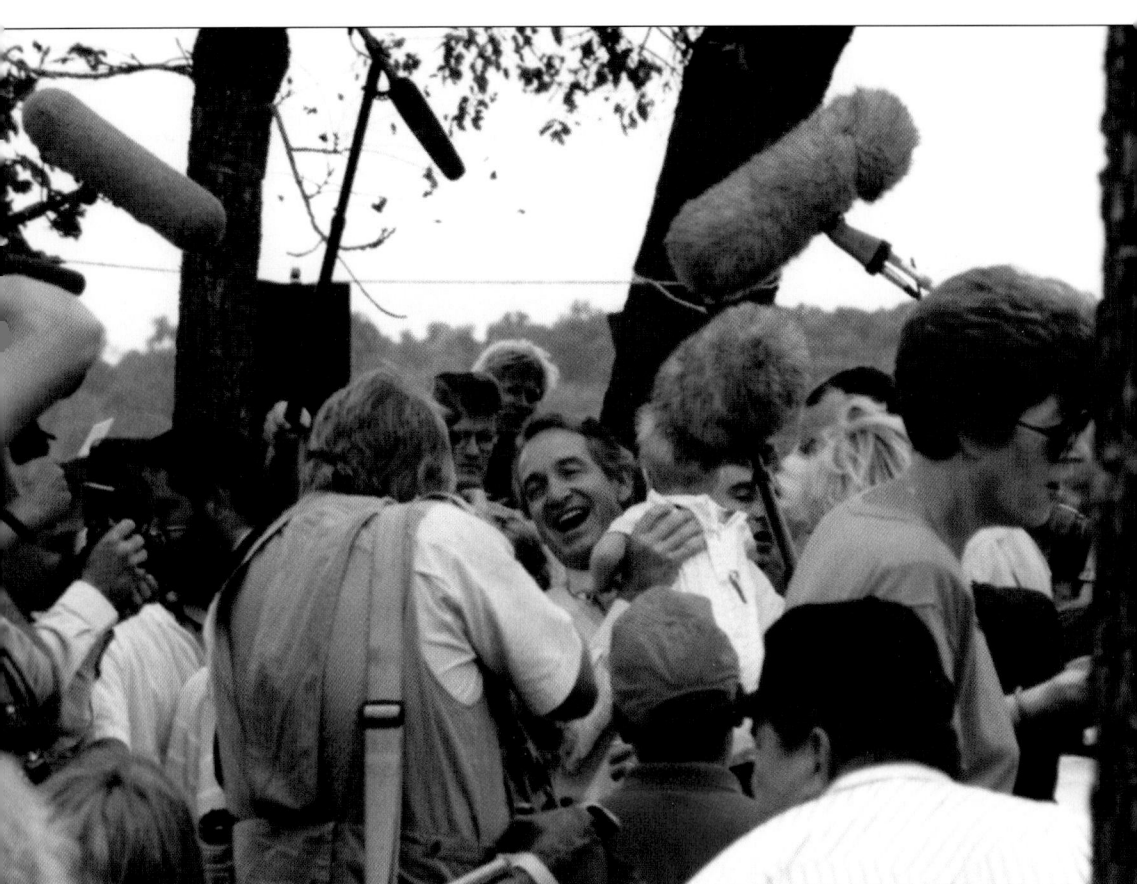

Tom Harkin declared his candidacy for the presidency at his annual steak fry in 1991 in Winterset, Iowa. As an Iowa senator, Harkin did not need to introduce himself to Democratic voters, and few other Democrats (including Bill Clinton) chose to compete for the nod in the Iowa caucuses. Harkin won an overwhelming 76 percent support among Iowa Democrats. After a fourth-place finish in New Hampshire, Harkin went on to win the Idaho and Minnesota caucuses as well, but he ultimately dropped out of the race in early March 1992. With incumbent Republican president George H.W. Bush uncontested as well, 1992 was a slow campaign year in Iowa. (Courtesy of the Harkin Collection, Drake University Archives and Special Collections.)

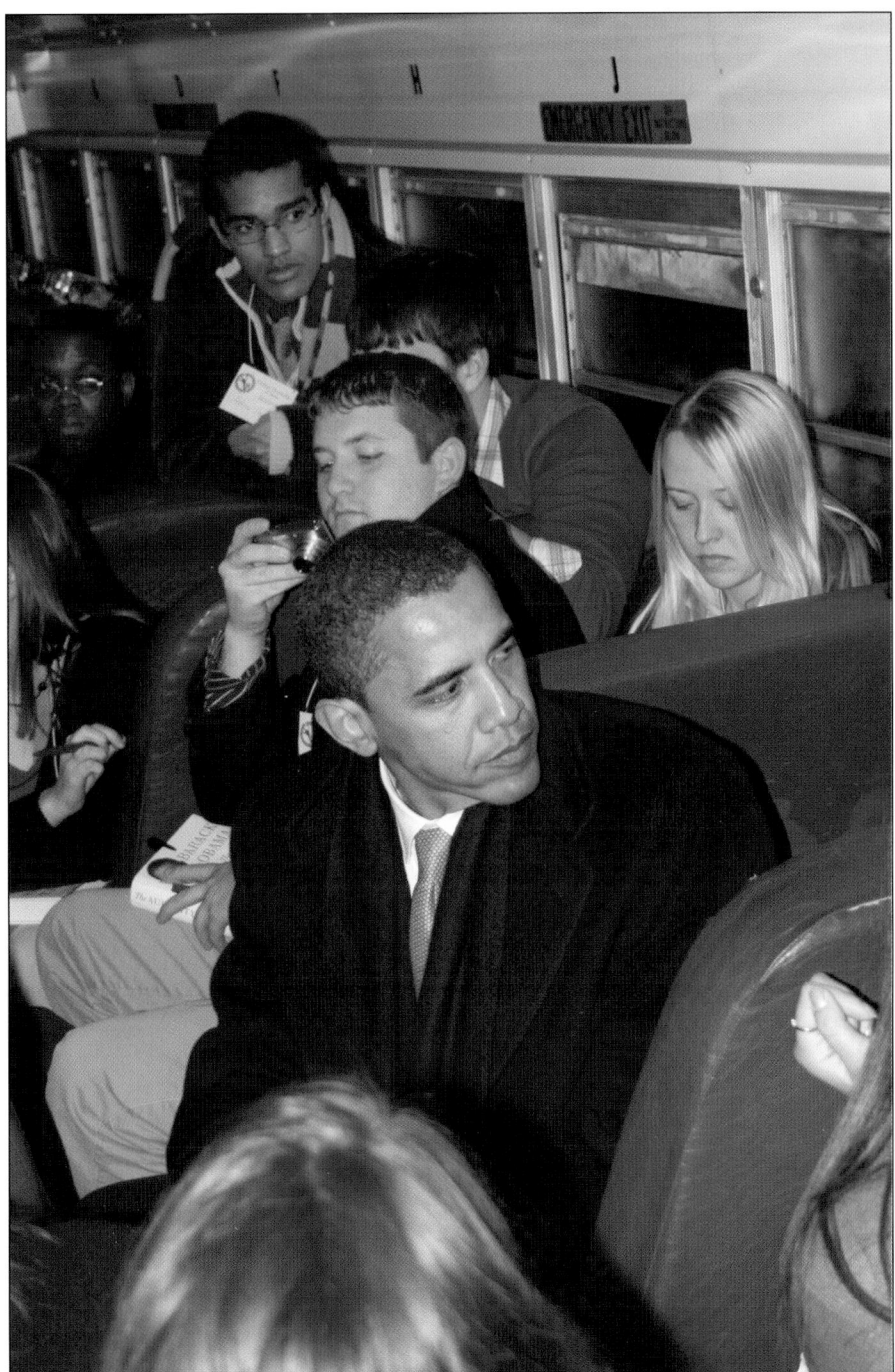

In Iowa, activists and supporters can come in any form, including college students. Candidates often do small group events, but they also work with Iowa organizations to introduce themselves to activists. Sen. Barack Obama's campaign was particularly focused on young voters and first-time caucus-goers. In 2007, he joined a group of young Democrats for the bus ride to Waterloo for a campaign event. In the end, the grassroots organizing of the campaign paid off, and the Democrats had a record turnout on January 3, 2008. (Courtesy of Jordan Oster.)

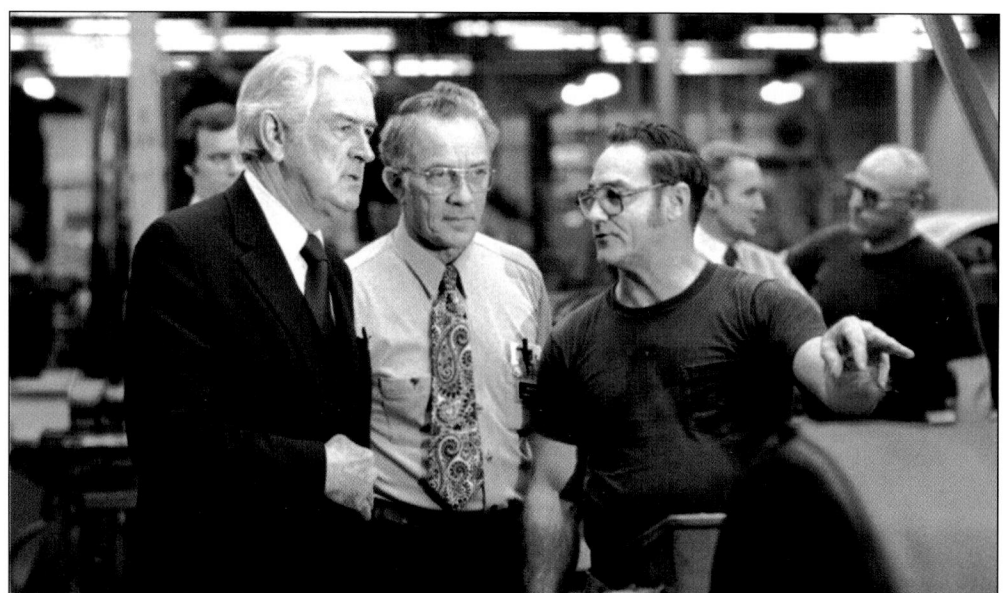

Former Texas governor John Connally, once a Democrat who served as treasury secretary under Pres. Richard Nixon, ran for the Republican nomination in 1980. Connally raised more money than other candidates, though rivals George H.W. Bush and Ronald Reagan concentrated on Iowa and Connally failed to break through in the state. Here, he meets with employees at the Firestone factory in Iowa. (Courtesy of the David Penney Collection, State Historical Society of Iowa, Des Moines.)

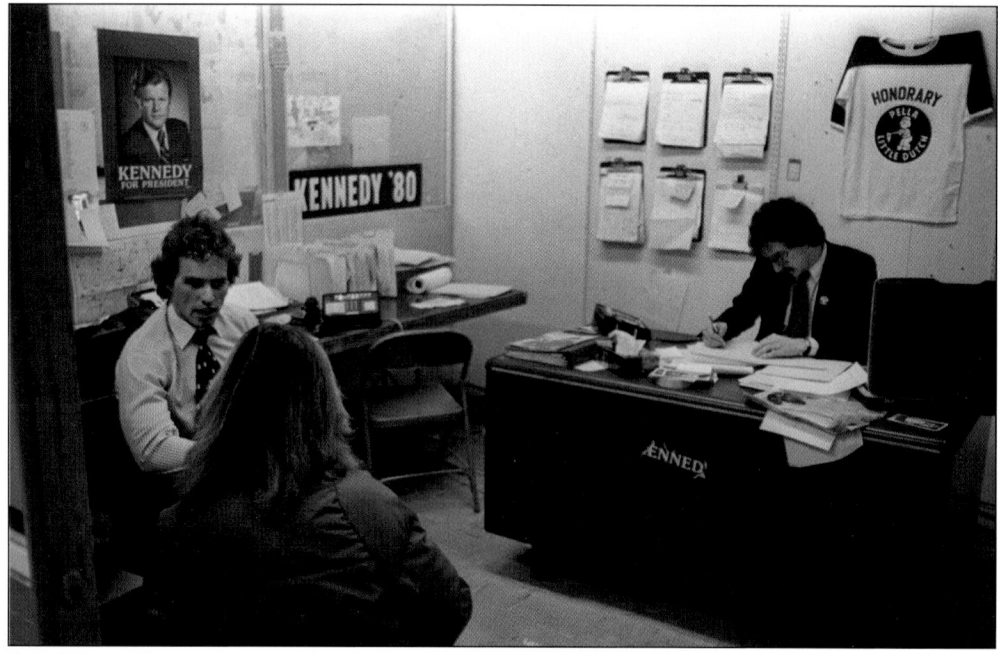

Candidate offices in Iowa tend to be haphazardly organized. Edward "Ted" Kennedy launched an unanticipated run against incumbent Jimmy Carter for the 1980 nomination. In this small office, the T-shirt on the wall reads, "Honorary Pella Little Dutch," referencing the local football team in Pella, Iowa. (Courtesy of the Harkin Collection, Drake University Archives and Special Collections.)

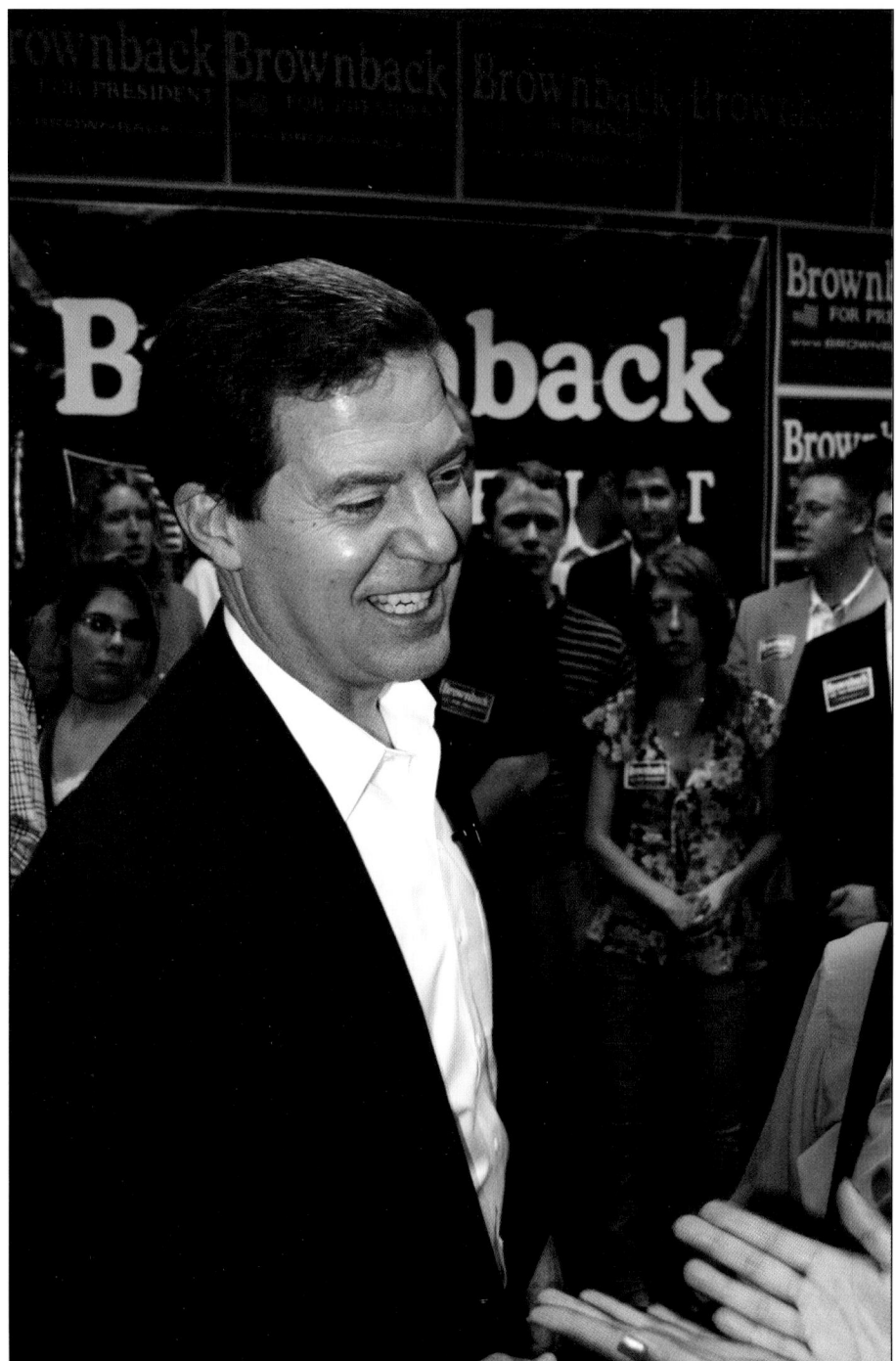

As candidates begin the process of establishing a presence in Iowa, the office opening is a critical early sign that the campaign is organizationally viable. Sen. Sam Brownback (R-KS) opened his office in May 2007. After a disappointing third-place finish in the Iowa Straw Poll demonstrated a lack of organizational capacity, Brownback's campaign lost strength, and he withdrew in October. (Courtesy of Jordan Oster.)

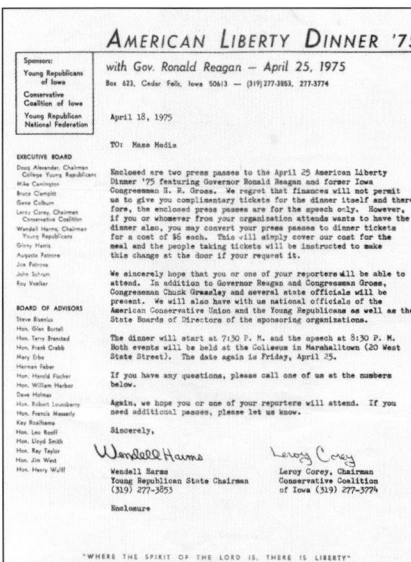

The 1975 American Liberty Dinner featured California governor Ronald Reagan, who was competing for the Republican nomination in 1976 against incumbent Gerald Ford. This letter details the plans for attendees, noting that members of the media will not receive a complementary dinner, but the organizers remain hopeful that reporters will attend. The mass media is now a regular fixture at nearly every candidate appearance, and campaigns spend a good deal of time and energy to accommodate media attendance. (Courtesy of Frank Nye Papers, University of Iowa Libraries, Iowa City, Iowa.)

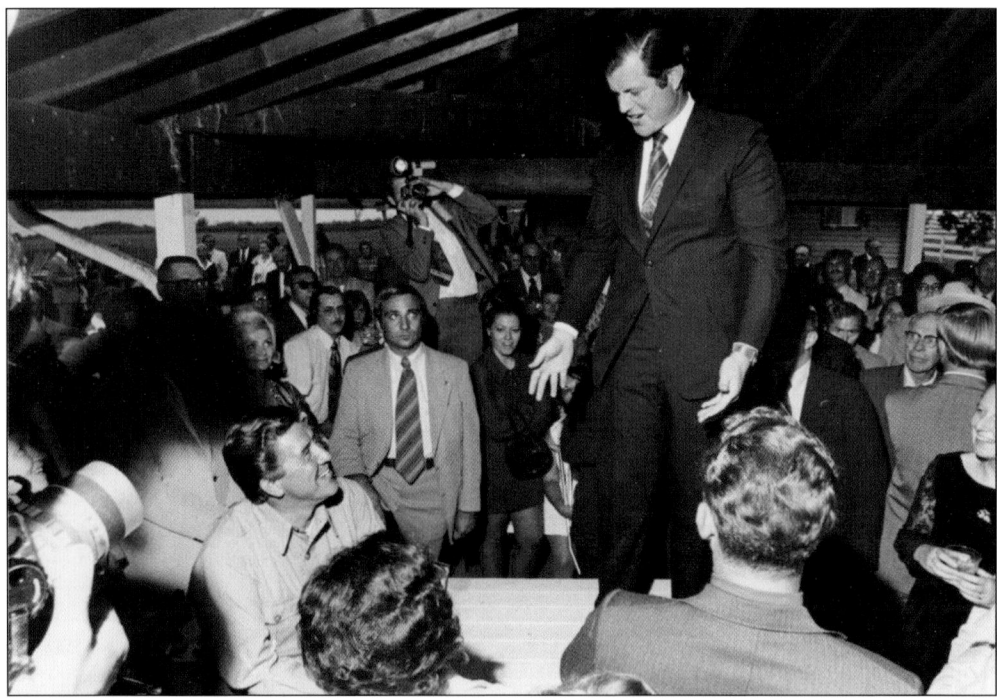

Massachusetts senator Edward Kennedy came to Iowa to campaign with Iowa senator Dick Clark in 1972 as the new caucus rules were coming into effect. The Chappaquiddick incident had badly damaged Kennedy's national reputation, but he remained a popular potential candidate and considered a run for the White House. By June 1972, groups opposing McGovern attempted to persuade Kennedy to enter the race, but he refused. By the time of the national convention, McGovern had tried to get Kennedy to join the ticket, only to be declined. Kennedy went on to run for the presidency in 1980 against incumbent Jimmy Carter, though Carter won more than twice the support of Kennedy in the caucuses. (Courtesy of the Dick Clark Papers, University of Iowa Libraries, Iowa City, Iowa.)

Two

MEETING AND GREETING LARGE AND SMALL

Every four years, the nation turns its eyes to Iowa for the first-in-the-nation caucuses. Although national media covers the caucuses, they rarely offer a glimpse of the many diverse events that occur leading up to caucus night. Reporters are often corralled onto press risers and designated media placements to get just the right image for the camera. National broadcasts feature pundits talking about candidates and campaigns without much mention of the relationships that are built in Iowa or the people who turn out to vote on a cold evening in January or February.

For years before any votes are cast, candidates come to Iowa to meet party leaders, local activists, and average Iowa voters. Initial forays into Iowa frequently include a cadre of political strategists and small-town party activists, many of whom are never known outside of Iowa. Some are well-established local voices and prestigious community leaders; others are newly minted college graduates who have developed a reputation for hard work and dedication to the cause. A candidate's success will depend upon strong organization and networks of grassroots support across the state, allowing anyone—from a senator to a PTA member—to become an important and valued addition to the campaign team.

As the campaign season begins in earnest, which can happen 8 to 10 months ahead of the caucuses and long before the national audience tunes in, campaigns organize public events, seeking to attract a broader range of people to the campaign. These public events provide opportunities for candidates to meet and greet the voters in venues large and small. Candidates visit small-town diners, bars, restaurants, VFW halls, libraries, community centers, senior centers, parks, schools, businesses, farmers' markets, party fundraisers, and the homes of local campaign supporters. At each stop, the candidate interacts with voters, shaking hands, taking photographs, answering questions, and allowing voters to get to know who they are and what they think about the issues.

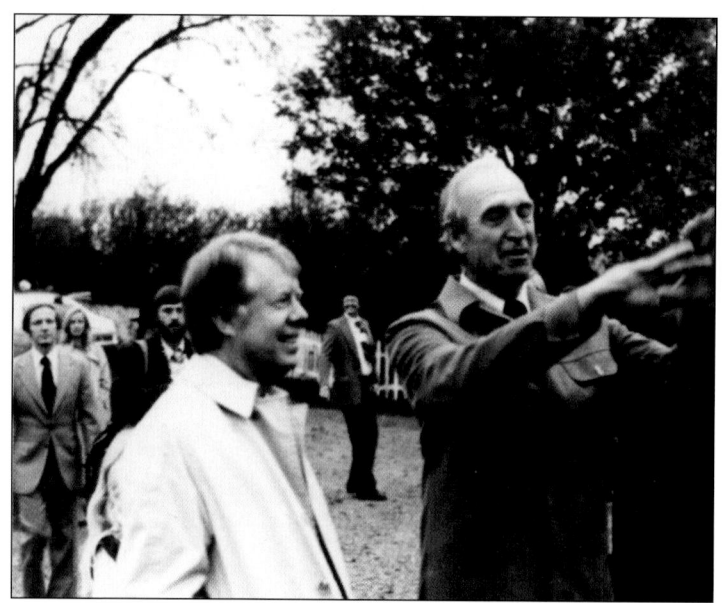

Jimmy Carter's 1976 campaign for the Iowa caucus created the standard model of retail politics, putting the state's first-in-the-nation status on the map. Here, Carter returns to the state prior to the 1980 election. While he had only won 27 percent support (coming in second) in 1976, he proved to be the big winner in 1980 with 59 percent of the vote. (Courtesy of the Harkin Collection, Drake University Archives and Special Collections.)

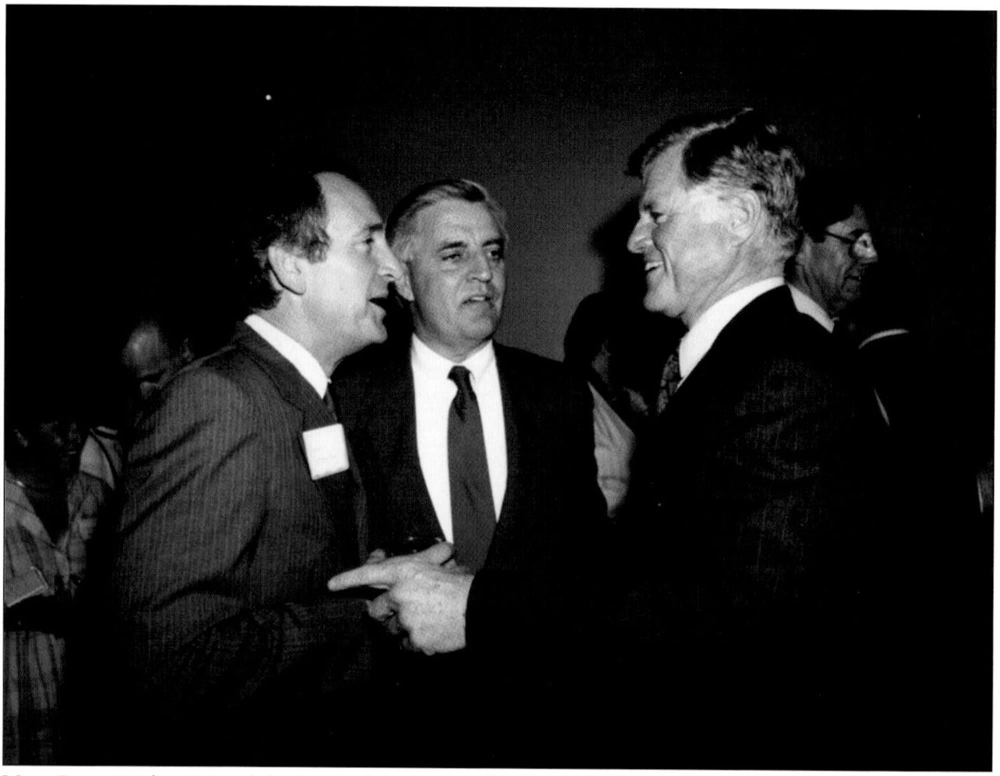

Vice Pres. Walter Mondale (center) is pictured here with Edward Kennedy (D-MA) and Tom Harkin (D-IA) in 1980. Kennedy launched an unexpected campaign against incumbent Jimmy Carter in 1980, losing the Iowa caucus despite achieving 31 percent support. Mondale would go on to win the Iowa caucuses in 1984 with 49 percent of the vote. (Courtesy of the Harkin Collection, Drake University Archives and Special Collections.)

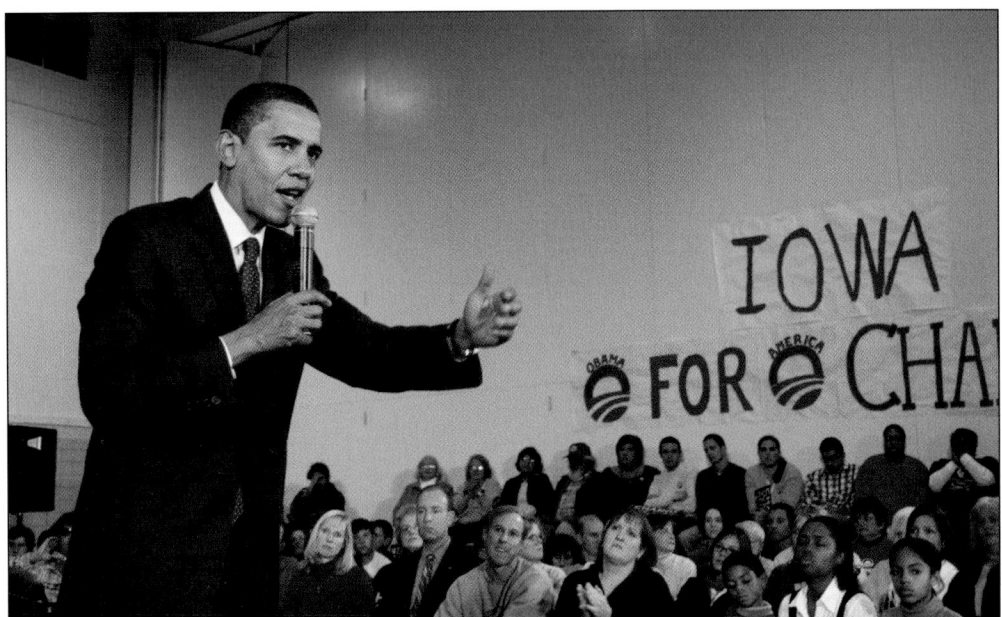

Sen. Barack Obama addresses a group of Iowa voters at North High School in Des Moines in 2007. A first-term senator who was virtually unknown until his 2004 Democratic National Convention address, Obama was considered a long shot for the Democratic nomination. His 2008 caucus-night victory propelled him to the presidency. (Courtesy of Jordan Oster.)

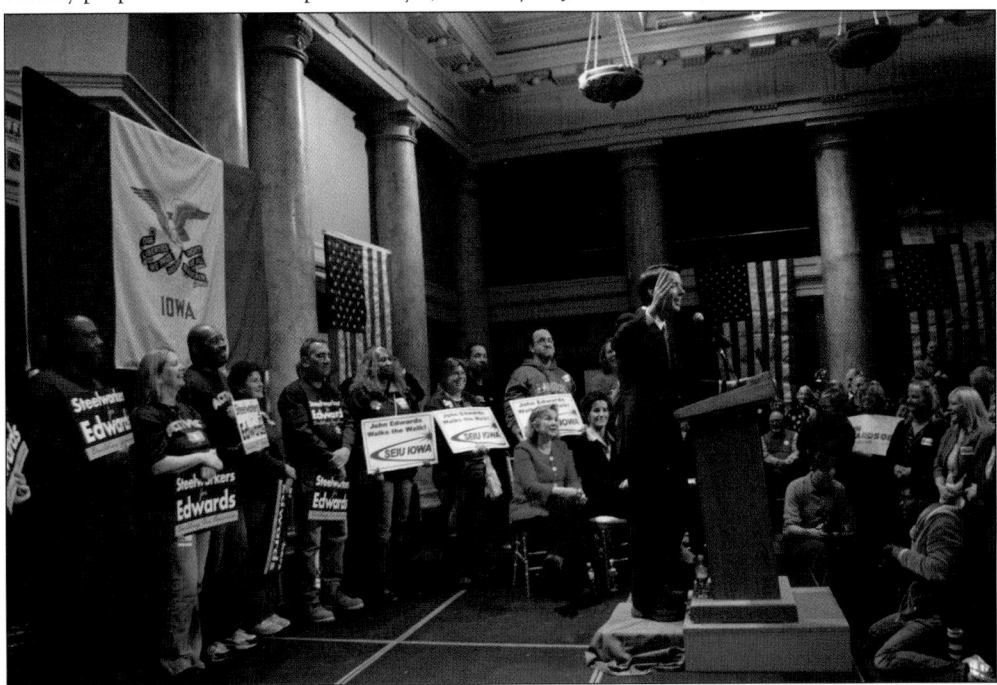

Campaigns use a variety of venues to hold small campaign events, and Iowa voters frequently serve as a backdrop for the candidate. John Edwards, pictured here at a 2007 campaign event with labor organizers, received substantial union support, though Barack Obama's 2008 operation proved superior on caucus night. (Courtesy of Jordan Oster.)

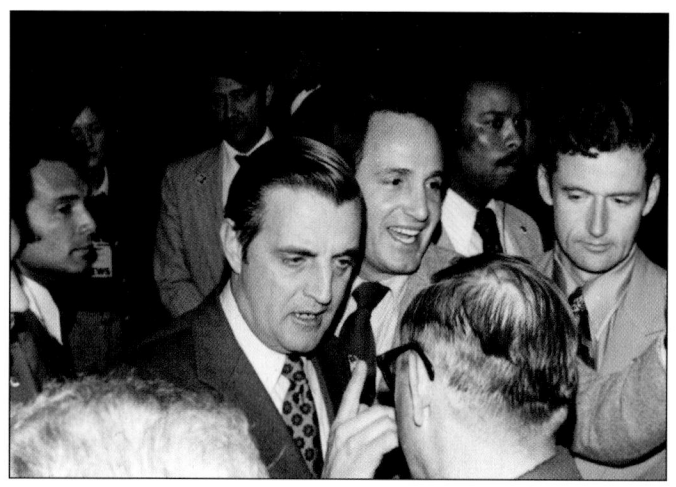

Walter Mondale spent a good deal of time in Iowa during his vice presidency. In 1984, he became the Democratic nominee after handily defeating his closest rival, Gary Hart, in the Iowa caucus. That would be the last time a winner of the Democratic caucuses went on to become the party nominee until 1996. (Courtesy of the Harkin Collection, Drake University Archives and Special Collections.)

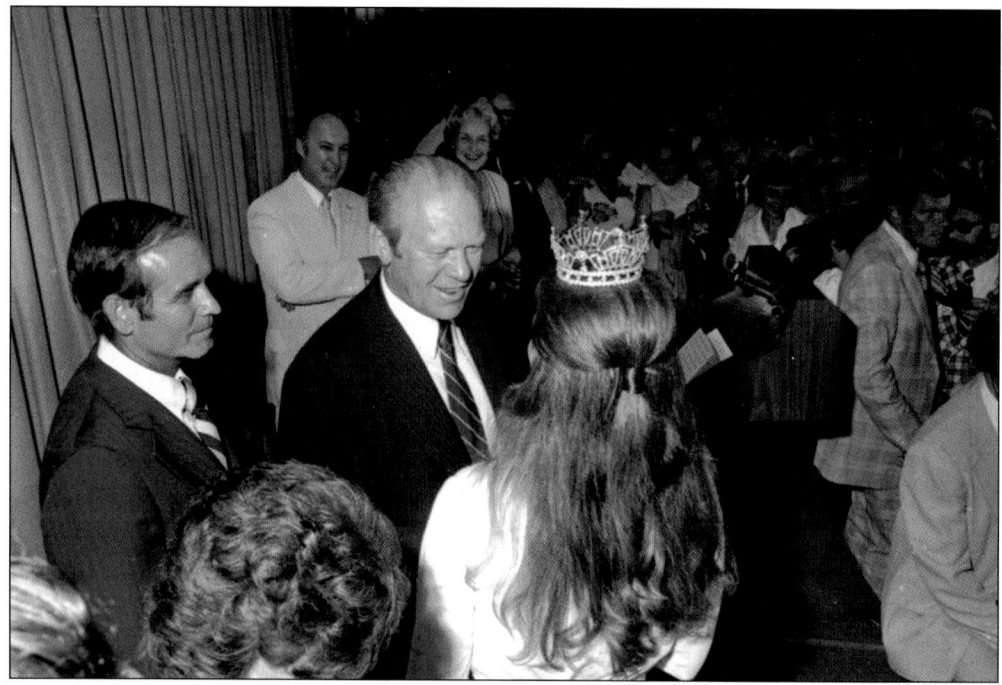

Pres. Gerald Ford, who entered the oval office upon the resignation of Pres. Richard Nixon, campaigned for the Republican nomination in Iowa. Ford visited Iowa several times in 1975, recognizing that competitor Ronald Reagan was a serious contender among the more conservative base. On caucus night, Ford bested Reagan 45 percent to 43 percent. Ford went on to win the nomination, replacing Nelson Rockefeller with Bob Dole as his running mate. (Courtesy of the David Penney Collection, State Historical Society of Iowa, Des Moines.)

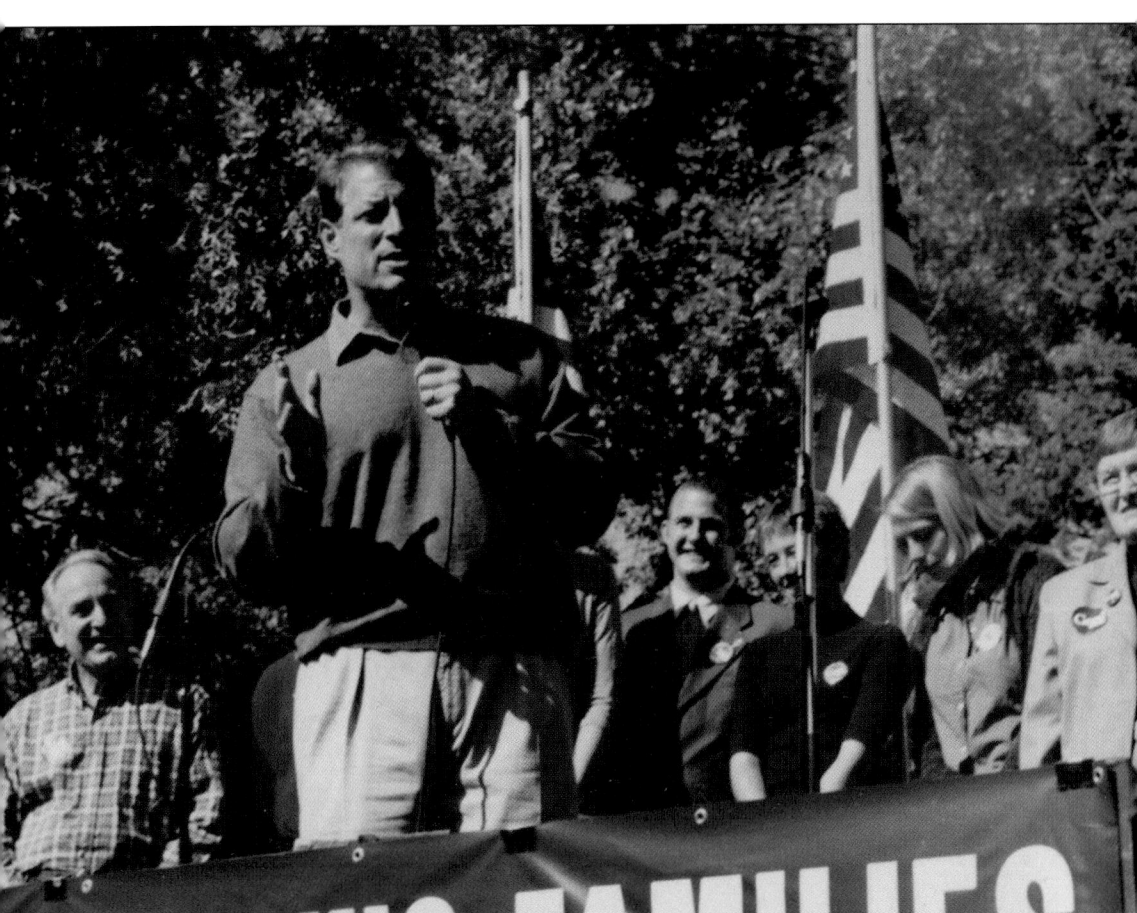

Vice Pres. Al Gore visits Iowa State University in 1999, when he was competing for the presidency. The Democrats had a quiet decade in the 1990s given Tom Harkin's home-state advantage in 1992 and Bill Clinton's reelection effort in 1996. Despite a challenge from Bill Bradley (D-NJ), Gore's extensive Iowa connections during the Clinton-Gore administration proved helpful in his presidential effort—he won the caucuses with 63 percent of the vote over his only competitor, Bill Bradley. Gore went on to win every state primary or caucus but lost the general election to George W. Bush. (Courtesy of the Harkin Collection, Drake University Archives and Special Collections.)

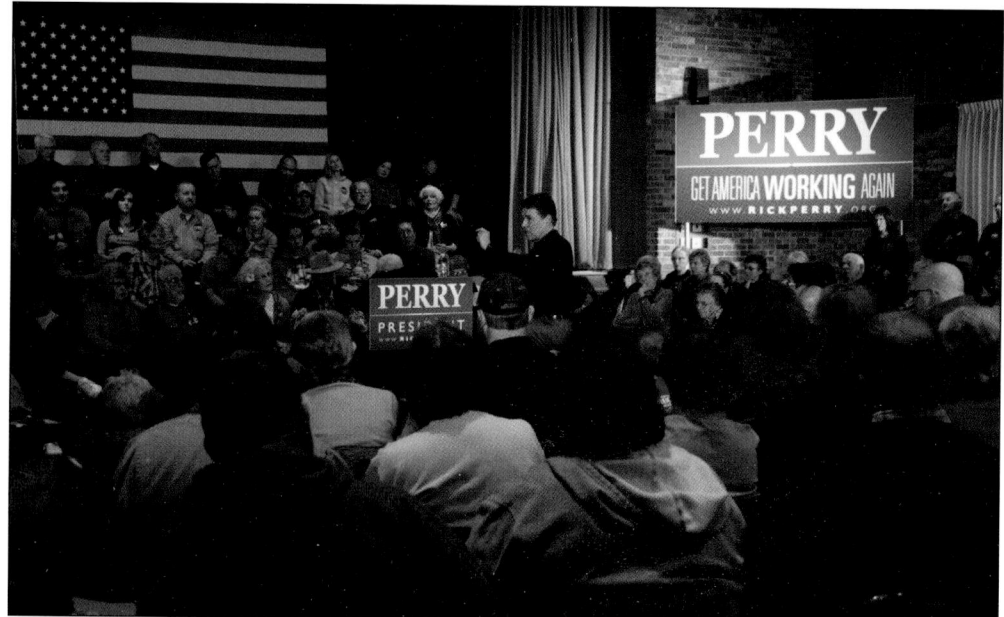

Rick Perry takes questions from an audience in Boone, Iowa, prior to the 2012 Republican caucuses. With President Obama running for reelection, the Republicans had the spotlight in 2012, with 12 major candidates ultimately joining the race. Texas governor Rick Perry struggled to find his footing in Iowa, summing up his experience by saying that he had underestimated the difficulty of the Iowa campaign. (Author's collection.)

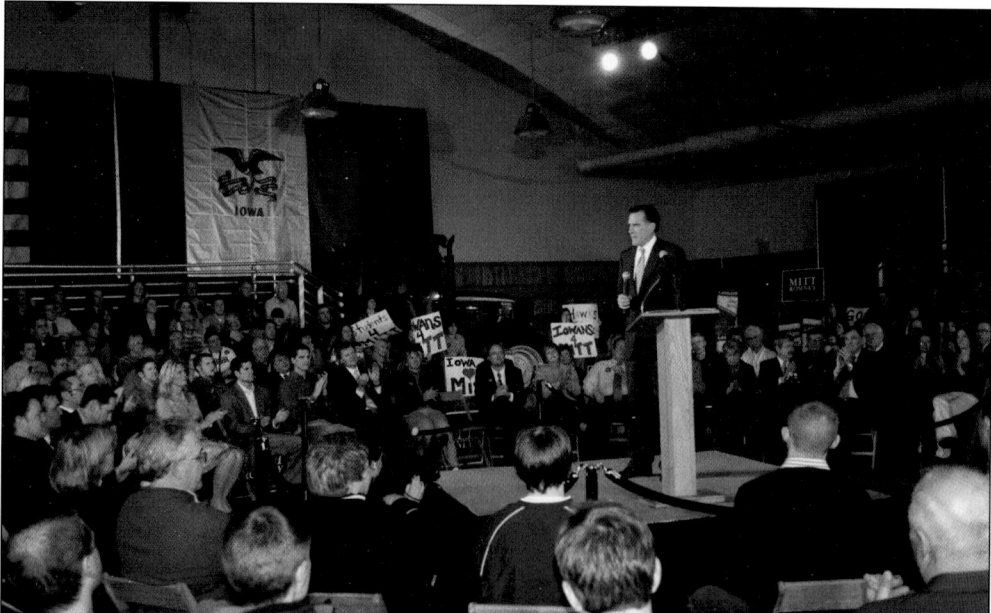

The green-and-yellow John Deere tractor is a widely used Iowa icon (the John Deere Museum is located in Waterloo). Here, Mitt Romney uses the Iowa flag and the tractor at an indoor event during his announcement tour in February 2007. Eleven months later, he was bested by Mike Huckabee in the Iowa caucus, and John McCain ultimately won the Republican nomination. (Courtesy of Jordan Oster.)

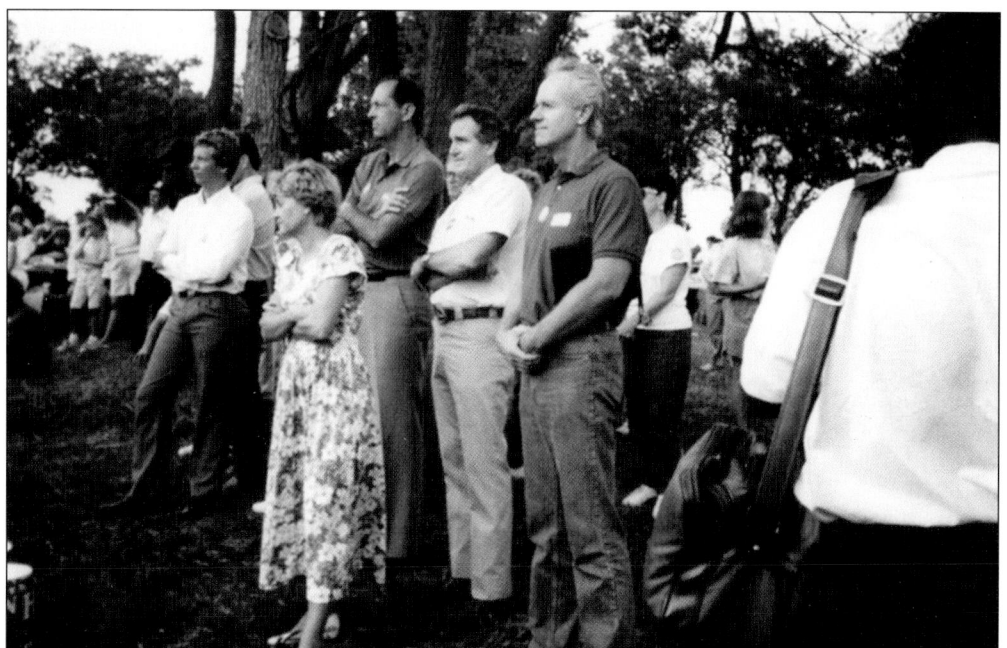

Many would-be candidates come to Iowa early and often. Here, Sen. Bill Bradley (D-NJ) (third from right) looks on at a Democratic fundraiser in Iowa in 1990. Bradley unexpectedly challenged sitting–vice president Al Gore for the Democratic nomination in 2000. (Courtesy of the Harkin Collection, Drake University Archives and Special Collections.)

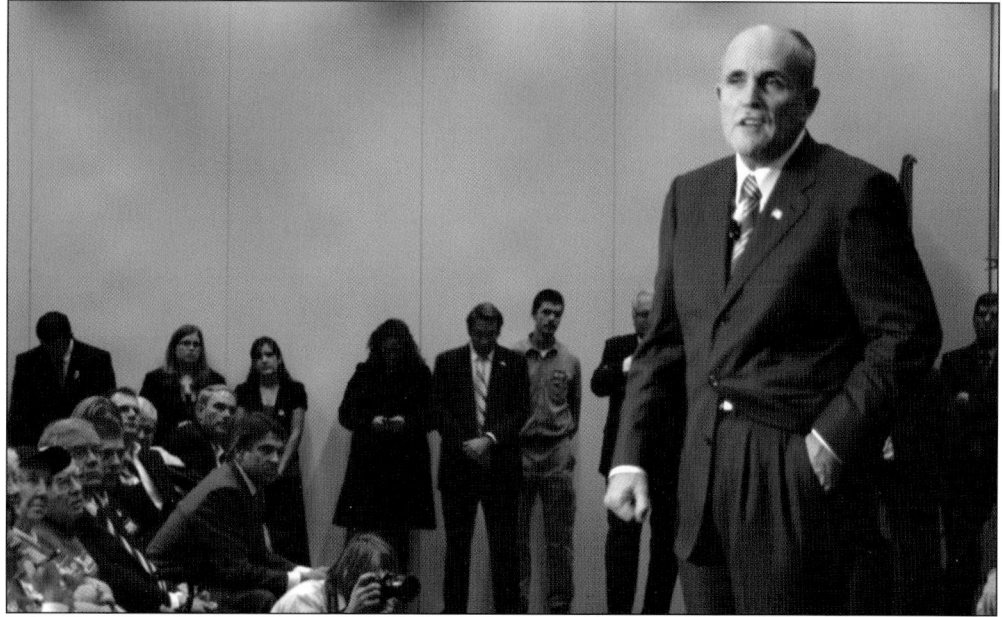

Following the September 11, 2001, attacks on the World Trade Center, New York Mayor Rudy Giuliani, seen here at a 2007 event at Drake University, was the prohibitive front-runner for the Republican Party nomination in 2008 to follow the presidency of George W. Bush. His liberal views on issues such as abortion did not endear him to Iowa's social conservatives, and he attracted just four percent of the vote in the caucuses on January 3, 2008. (Author's collection.)

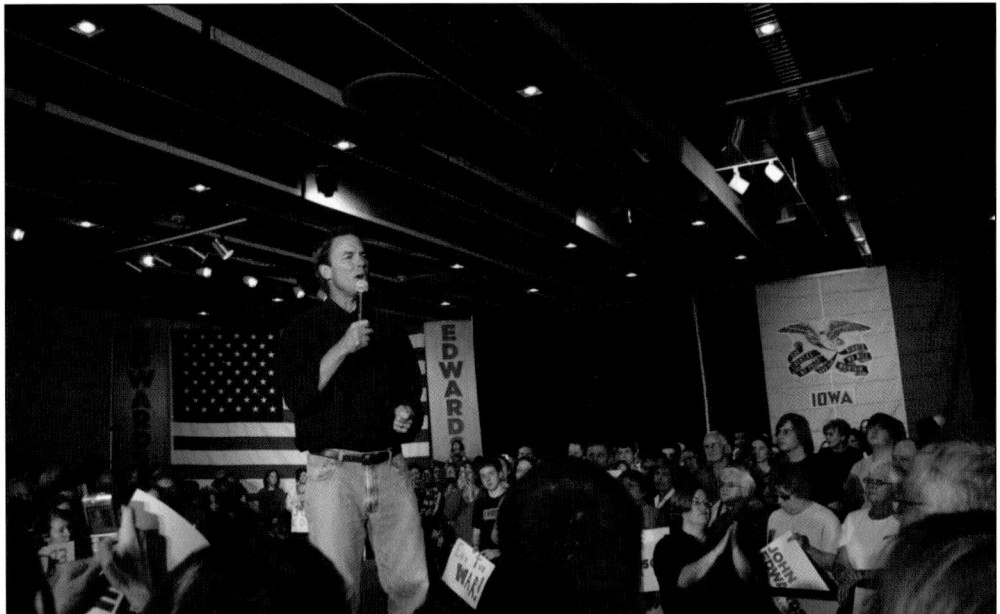

John Edwards, seen here at a campaign rally in 2003, ran for president in 2004 based on a message of "two Americas." He achieved an unexpectedly strong second place in the caucuses behind John Kerry and was later named as Kerry's running mate. In 2008, he achieved another second-place win behind Barack Obama. Shortly thereafter, it was discovered that he had been engaged in a long-term affair. (Courtesy of Jordan Oster.)

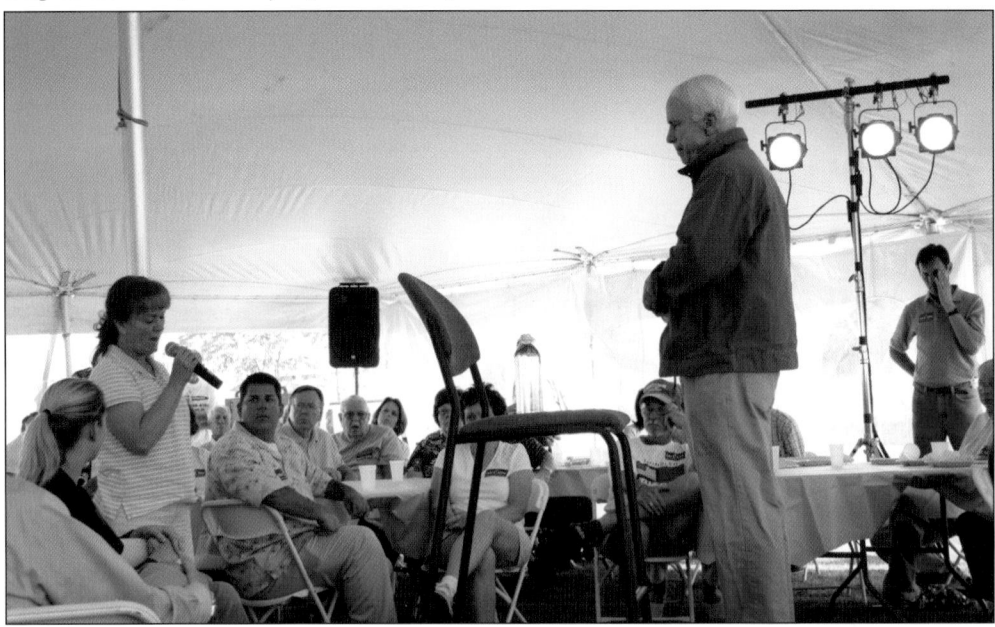

Arizona senator John McCain (appearing here at the Iowa State Fairgrounds in the summer of 2007) struggled on the campaign trail, virtually shutting down the campaign in late 2007. The downsized organization failed to capture the caucuses, and McCain came in fourth, with only 13 percent of the vote. He went on to win New Hampshire and became the Republican nominee for president. (Courtesy of Jordan Oster.)

With few staff members, little money, and the need to develop intensive voter outreach efforts, college students are often used as interns and field staff. Here, Sen. Joe Biden (D-DE) speaks with a small group of Drake University students during the first week of classes in 2006. Biden would go on to compete in the 2008 caucuses, eventually becoming vice president after losing the nomination to Barack Obama. (Courtesy of Jordan Oster.)

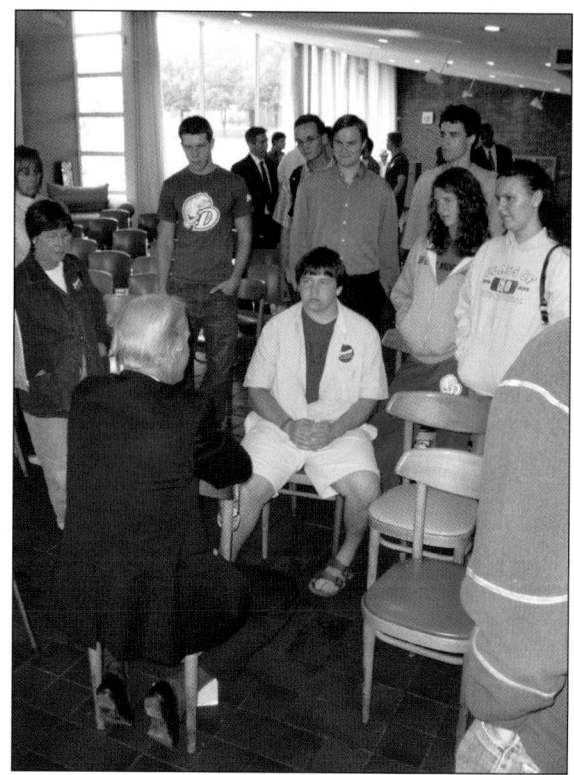

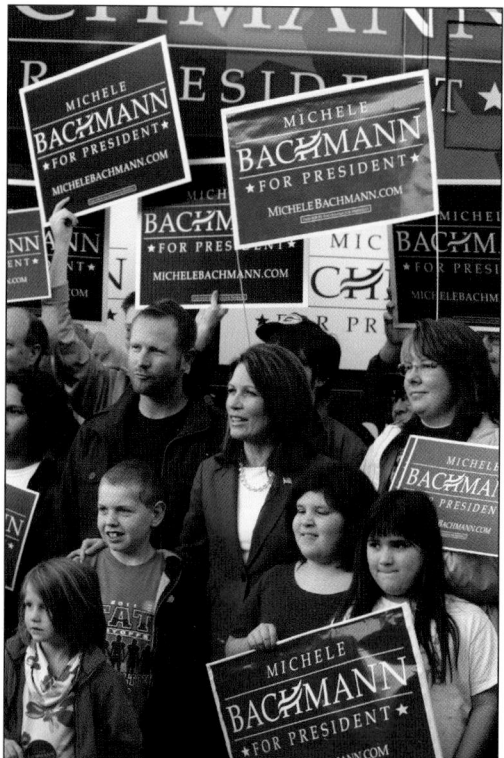

After a win at the Iowa Straw Poll, Minnesota representative Michele Bachmann's polling numbers declined during the fall of 2011. In an effort to demonstrate continued grassroots support, her campaign used campaign stops as an opportunity to film commercials from all 99 counties. Here, she gathers with supporters to shoot one of those commercials in Newton, Iowa, in the late fall of 2011. (Author's collection.)

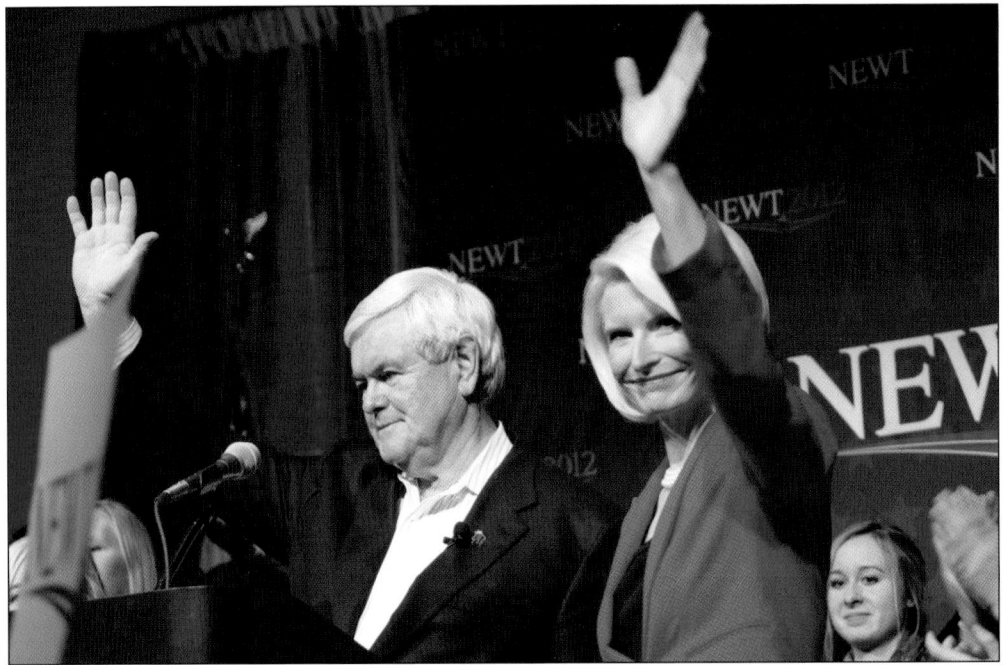

Former speaker of the house Newt Gingrich (R-GA) and his wife, Callista, speak to supporters on caucus night in 2012. Gingrich finished in fourth place with 13 percent of the vote despite briefly being the frontrunner in the fall of 2011. In a tumultuous race for the Republican nomination, many attribute his loss to poor debate showings. (Author's collection.)

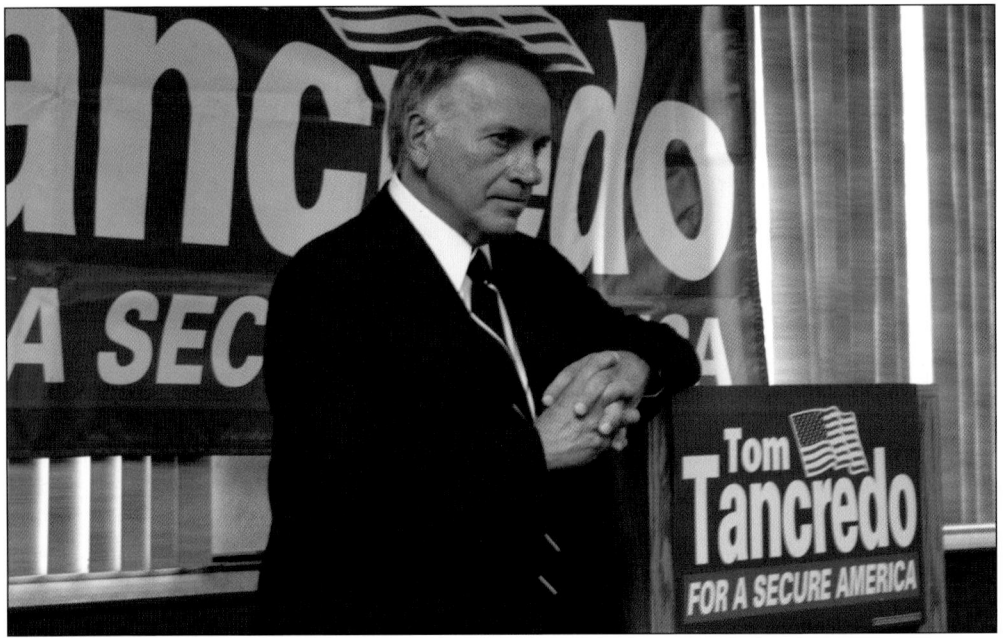

Many candidates enter the race with low poll ratings and little chance of winning the nomination. Tom Tancredo, a Republican congressman from Colorado, admitted that he was unlikely to win but hoped to engender debate about the issue of immigration. Two weeks prior to the 2008 caucus, he withdrew from the race and endorsed Mitt Romney. (Courtesy of Jordan Oster.)

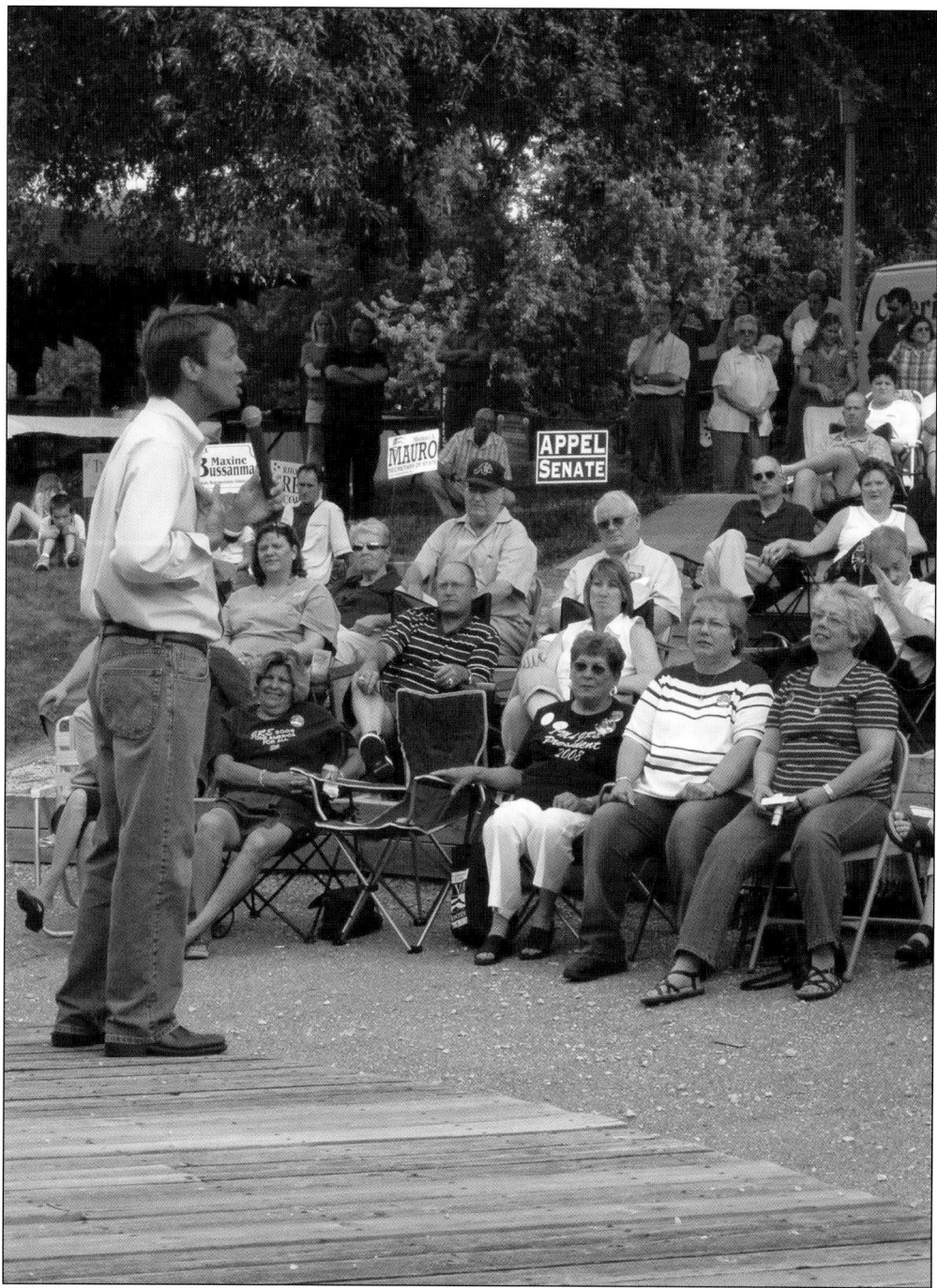

Each of Iowa's 99 counties has a party organization, and county party events provide opportunities for presidential candidates to introduce themselves. After a strong second-place finish in the 2004 Iowa caucuses and selection as John Kerry's 2004 running mate, John Edwards (pictured here at a Warren County Democrats picnic in 2006) maintained ties with county leaders and launched his 2008 campaign in December 2006, nearly two years before the general election. (Courtesy of Jordan Oster.)

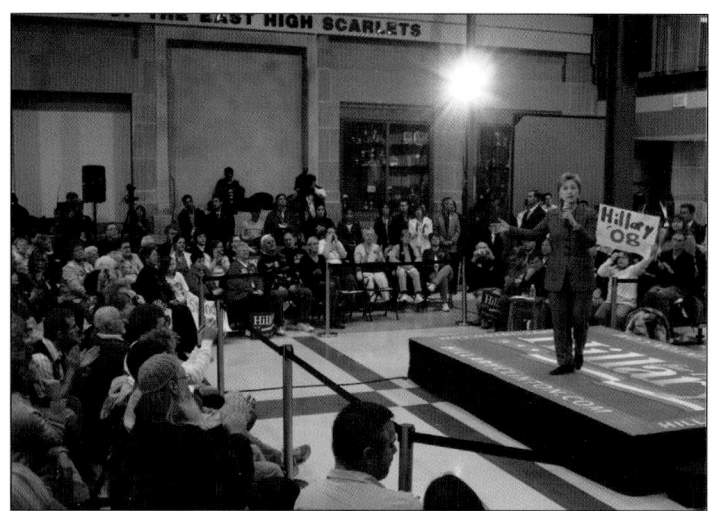

In Iowa, even large group events afford voters unusual proximity to candidates in relatively informal settings. Hillary Clinton's campaign events, like this one at East High School, were larger than most candidates'. She struggled to connect to Iowa voters and was beaten by Barack Obama and John Edwards in 2008. (Courtesy of Jordan Oster.)

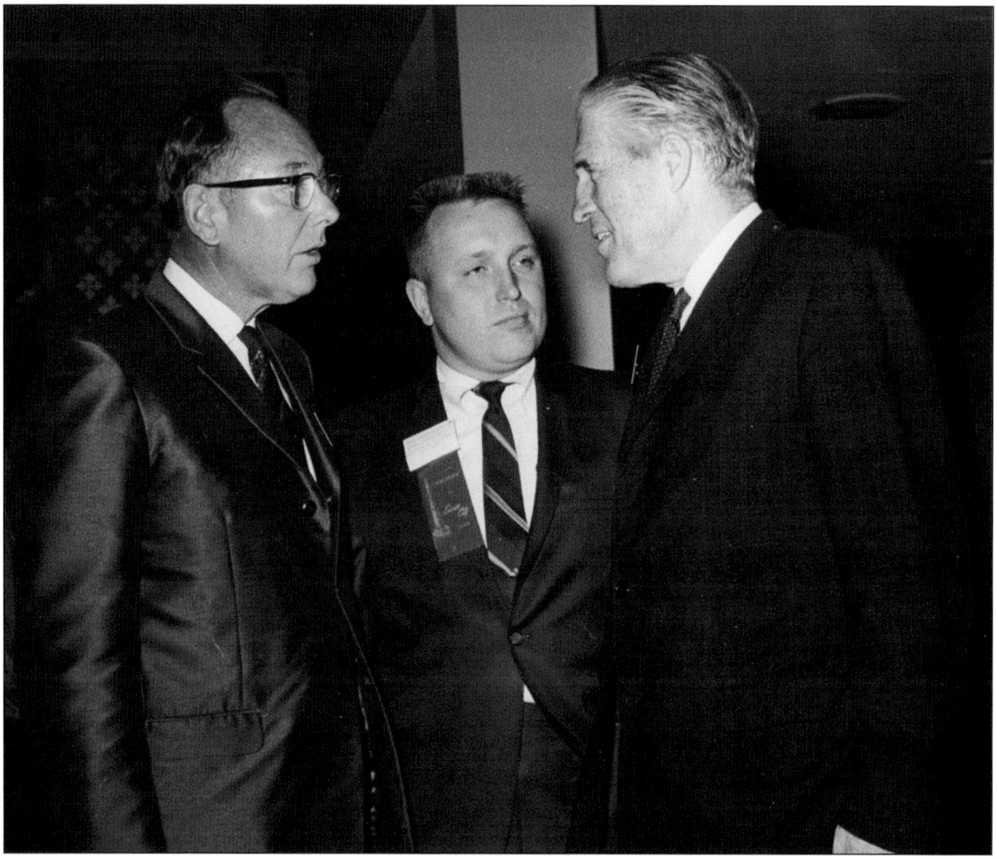

For many years, the Iowa congressional delegation organized the Sioux City Steak Dinner for notable politicos. Here, George Romney (right) attends the 1969 Sioux City Steak Dinner after his unsuccessful 1968 campaign. Romney was widely considered to be a likely candidate in future races, and the change in rules (both in Iowa and within the Democratic Party) would put Iowa in the first-in-the-nation position in 1972. (Courtesy of the Wiley Mayne Papers, University of Iowa Libraries, Iowa City, Iowa.)

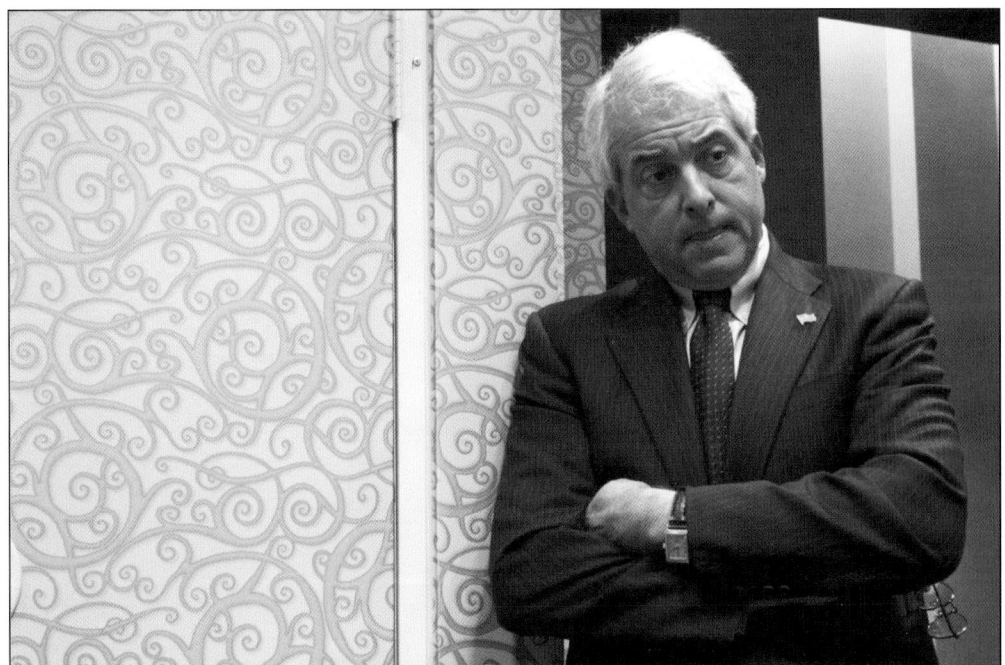

Iowa voters have the chance to meet all presidential candidates, even those who are unknown in other states. John Cox, a Chicago businessman, was the first to declare his candidacy for the 2008 Republican nomination. He withdrew from the race before the caucuses took place in part because events like this one in Des Moines attracted very small audiences; just three people showed up for this meet and greet. (Courtesy of Jordan Oster.)

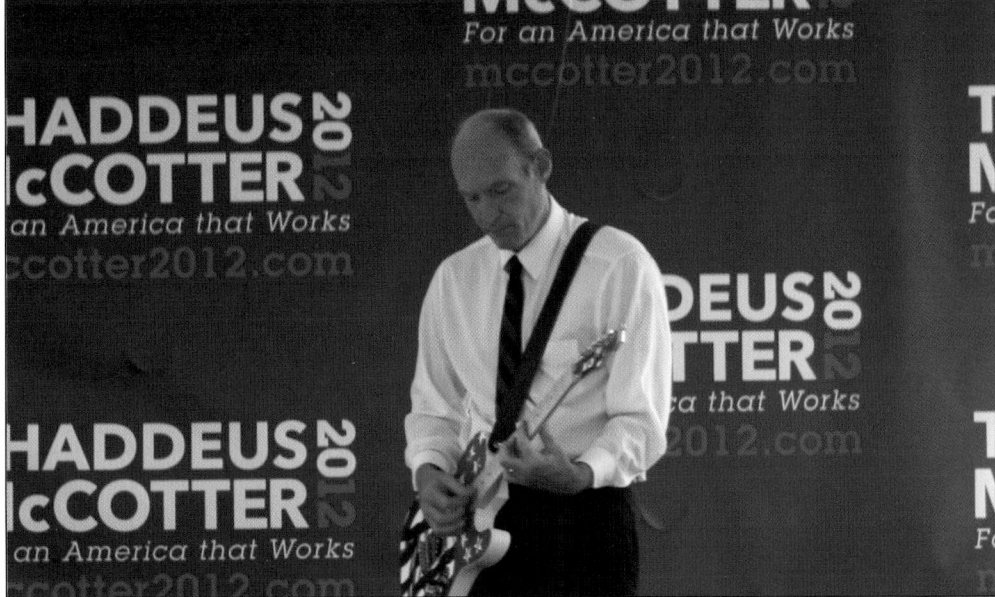

Congressman Thaddeus McCotter (R-MI) had a short-lived campaign for the Republican nomination in 2011. Basing his campaign on government reform, McCotter set up a stage at the Iowa Straw Poll and performed for attendees, though he came in last in the preference poll. He dropped out in early September. (Author's collection.)

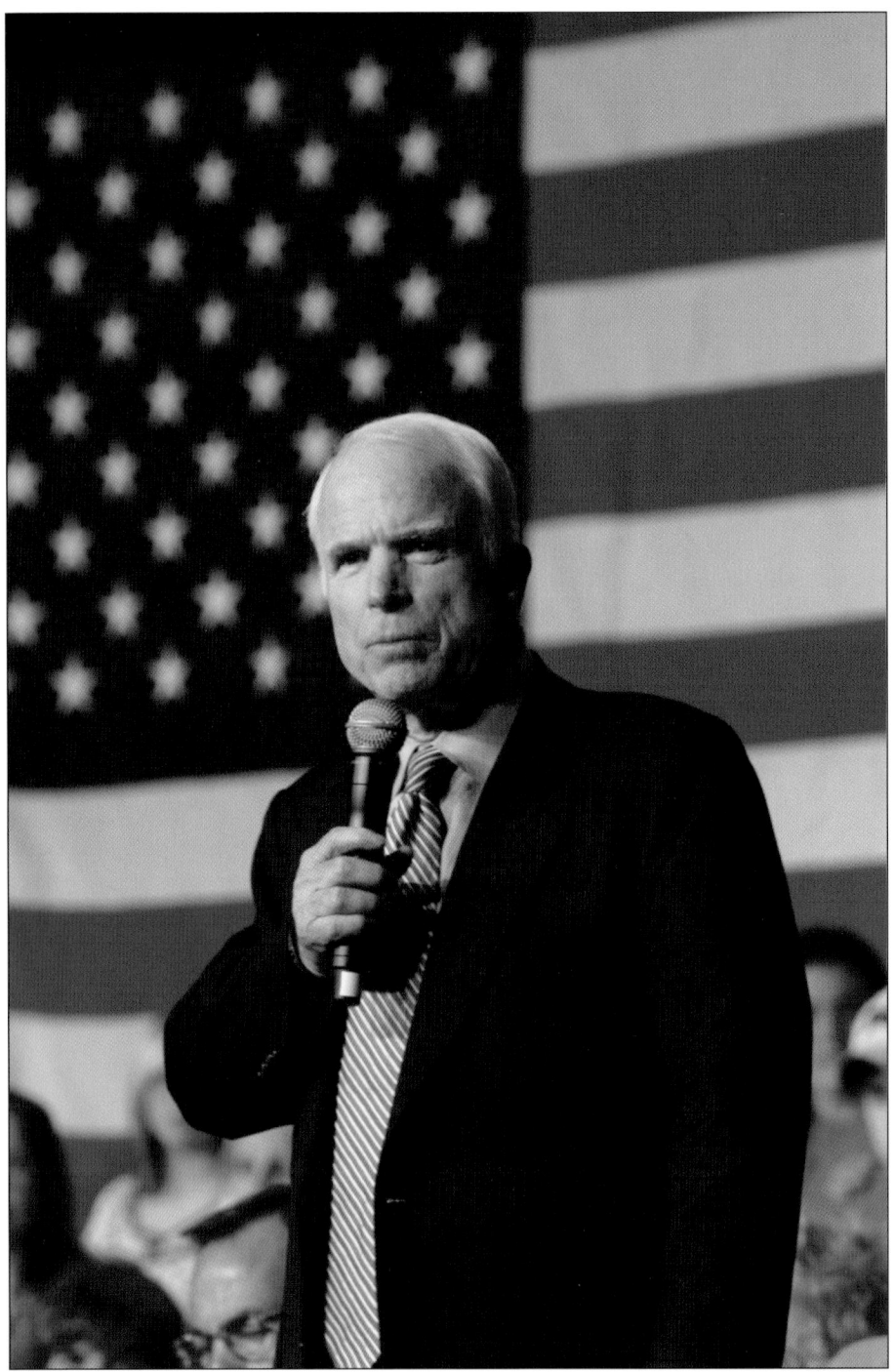

Arizona senator John McCain ran for president in 2000 and 2008, ultimately winning the nomination in 2008 despite pundits' claims that his campaign was over in the summer of 2007. While his 2000 *Straight Talk Express* bus positioned him as a self-described maverick, his 2008 campaign leaned toward the establishment. He tied for third place in the 2008 Republican caucuses, but a win in New Hampshire resurrected his campaign. (Courtesy of Jordan Oster.)

In an effort to meet as many Iowa voters as possible at multiple events, candidates often hold several branded events under a common theme. During his 2007 campaign, Mitt Romney conducted a series of "Ask Mitt Anything" town hall meetings. Here, he speaks with voters after one event. (Courtesy of Jordan Oster.)

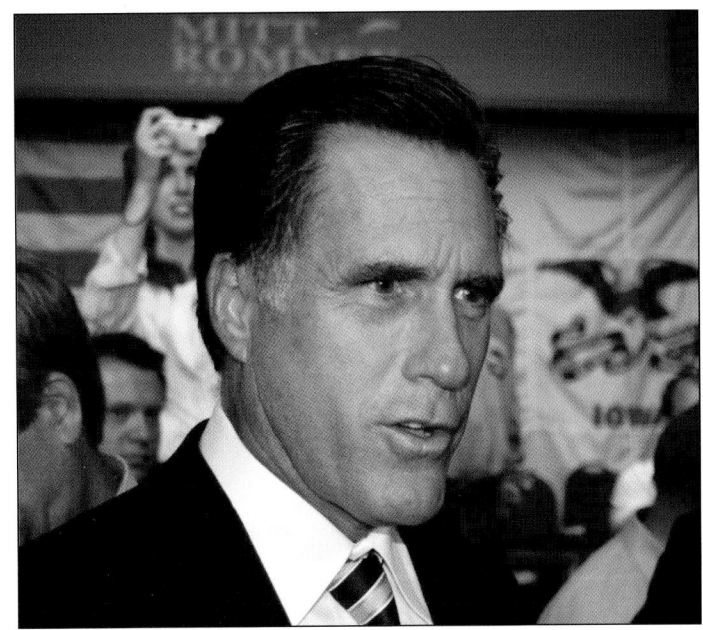

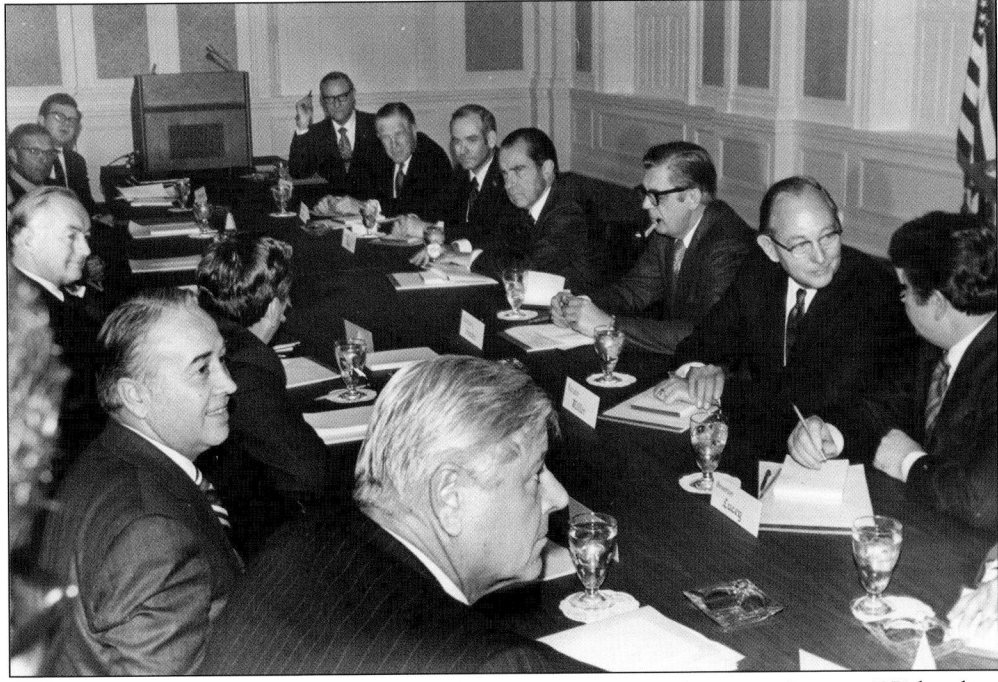

As president, Richard Nixon organized a Rural Development Conference in Iowa in 1971 heading into his 1972 reelection campaign. Guests included Congressman John Kyl (back row, far right; who would later be mentioned as a potential candidate), Secretary of Housing and Urban Development George Romney (back row, second from left; who had run in 1968 and was considered a potential future candidate), and White House staffer Donald Rumsfeld (back row, third from right; who would go on to become secretary of defense under Pres. Gerald Ford and under Pres. George W. Bush). The Republican caucus was not contested in 1972. (Courtesy of Wiley Mayne Papers, the University of Iowa Archives, Iowa City.)

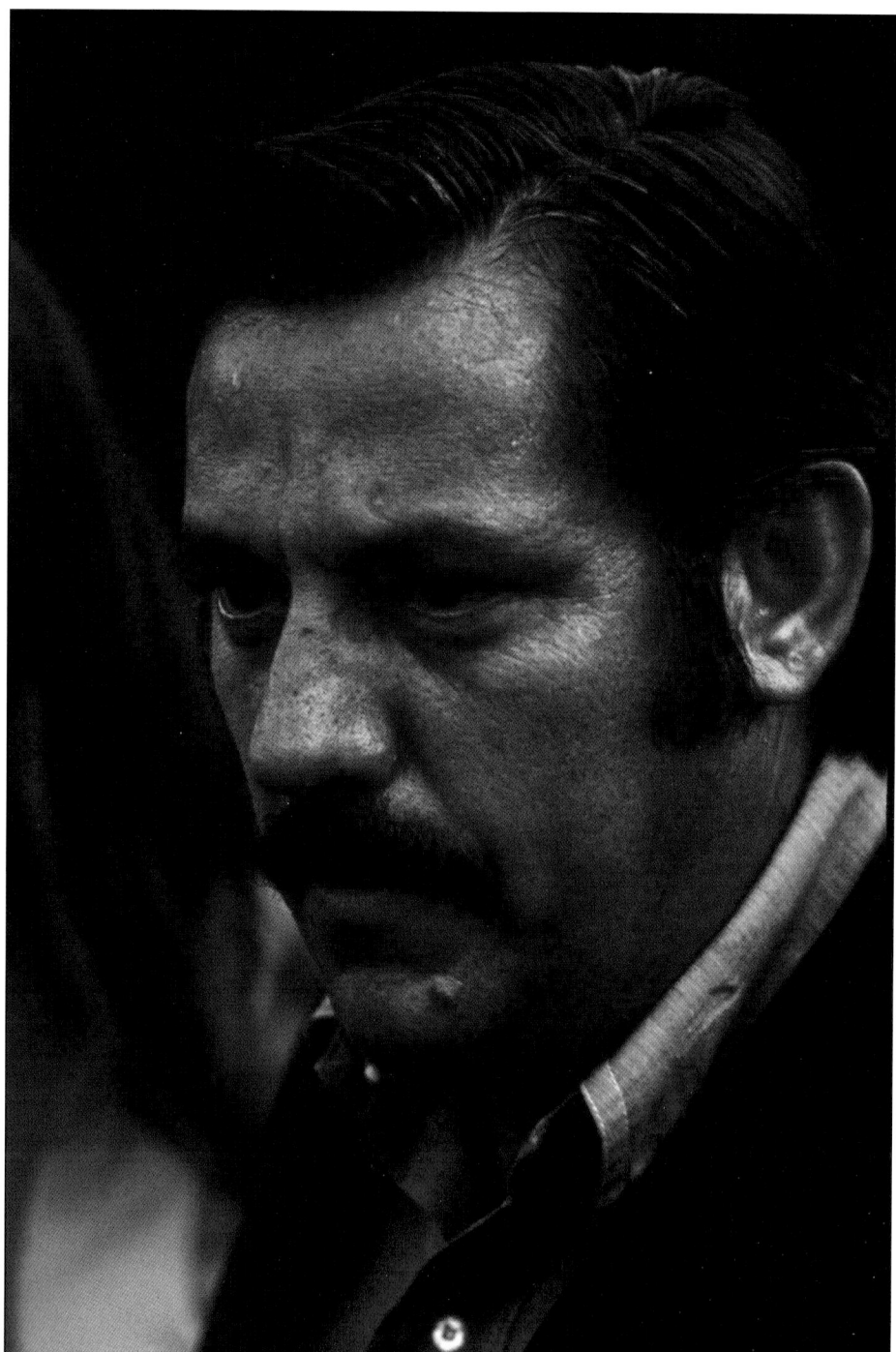

Although Jimmy Carter's 1976 presidential campaign in Iowa is well documented, few remember the campaign of Sen. Fred Harris (D-OK). Harris's campaign was run out of an RV, and he spent nights in supporters' homes. After a fourth-place finish, Harris said that he was "winnowed in" by the caucus, but it was Carter's unexpectedly strong second-place finish that garnered media attention. (Courtesy of Keith Wessel.)

During a little-known 2012 campaign for president as the first openly gay candidate, Fred Karger aimed to increase awareness of gay-rights issues. A political consultant who worked on nine Republican presidential campaigns, Karger recognized his long-shot status by using the slogan "Fred Who?" His campaign failed to register support in Iowa. (Author's collection.)

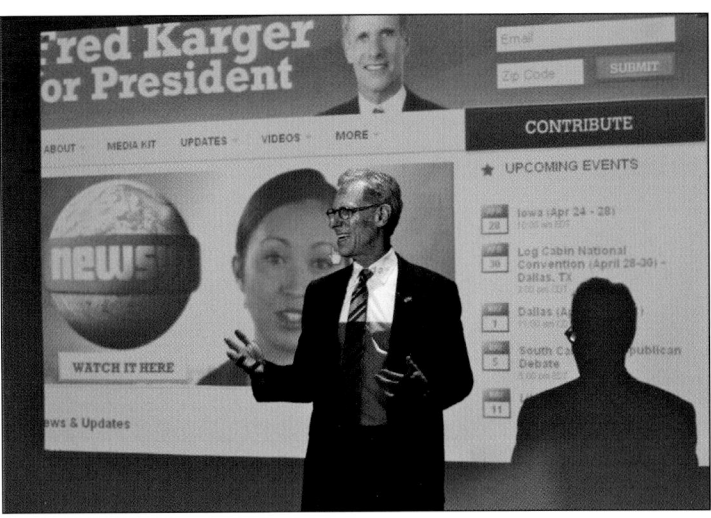

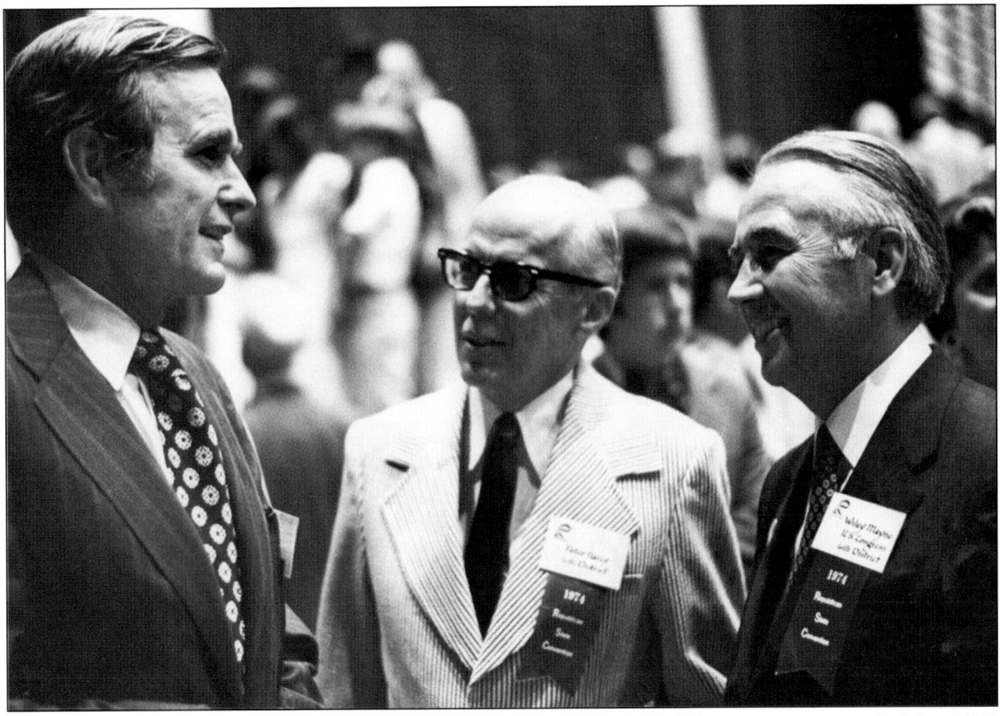

George Herbert Walker Bush, as chair of the Republican National Committee, attended the 1974 state party convention. The year 1976 would be the first competitive caucus under the new rules governing presidential nominations, and the Republican party was anxious to determine how the new system would structure the process. Incumbent Gerald Ford would go on to narrowly defeat Ronald Reagan in the 1976 Iowa caucuses; Bush would go on to narrowly defeat Ronald Reagan in the 1980 Iowa caucuses. (Courtesy of the Wiley Mayne Papers, University of Iowa Libraries, Iowa City, Iowa.)

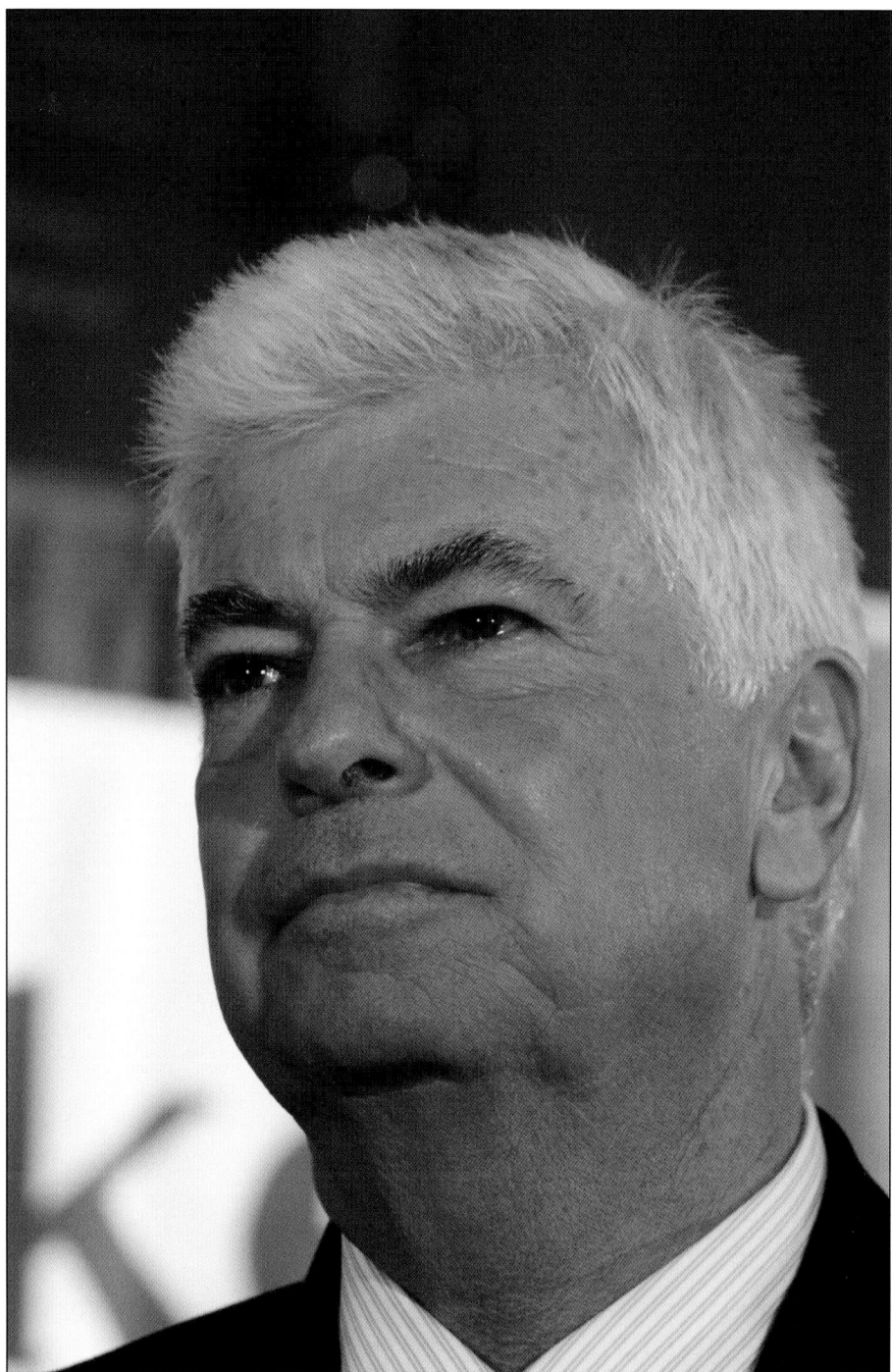

Serious candidates for the presidency know that spending time in Iowa is essential. But Sen. Chris Dodd (D-CT) took the tongue-in-cheek "you have to *live* in Iowa" to a new level when he purchased a home in Des Moines and relocated his family to the state, saying, "Chatting in a living room face to face is still a very important feature of campaigning here." He received zero percent of the vote on caucus night and withdrew from the race. (Courtesy of Jordan Oster.)

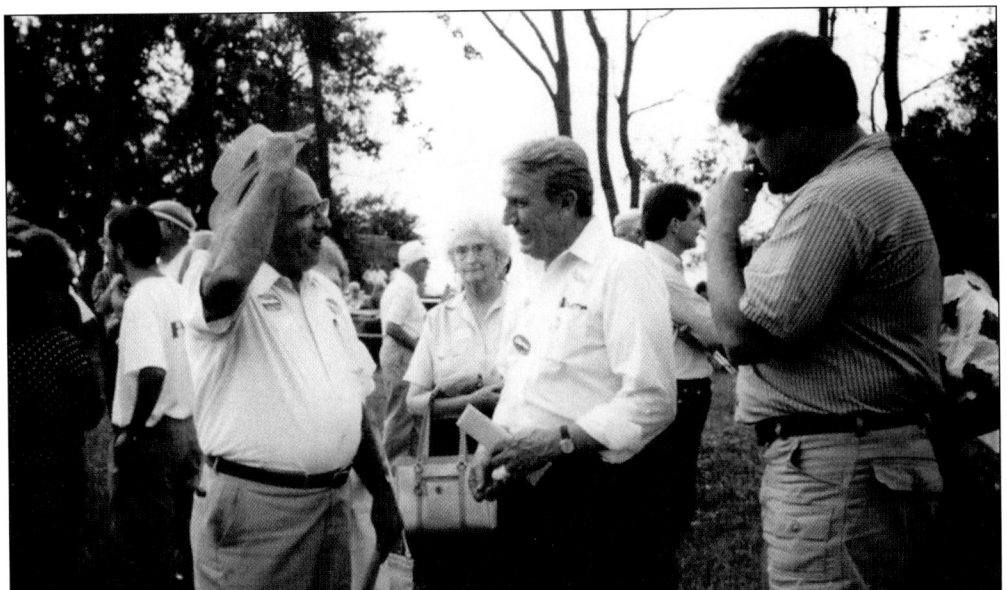

Would-be presidential candidates and those who have developed a national profile in the party often arrive to meet with voters in informal settings. Here, Dale Bumpers attends a Democratic campaign event in 1990 after ultimately deciding not to run for president in 1984 and 1988. Bumpers had been named as one of Walter Mondale's potential choices for the vice presidency in 1984, though he declared that he had no interest in the position. (Courtesy of the Harkin Collection, Drake University Archives and Special Collections.)

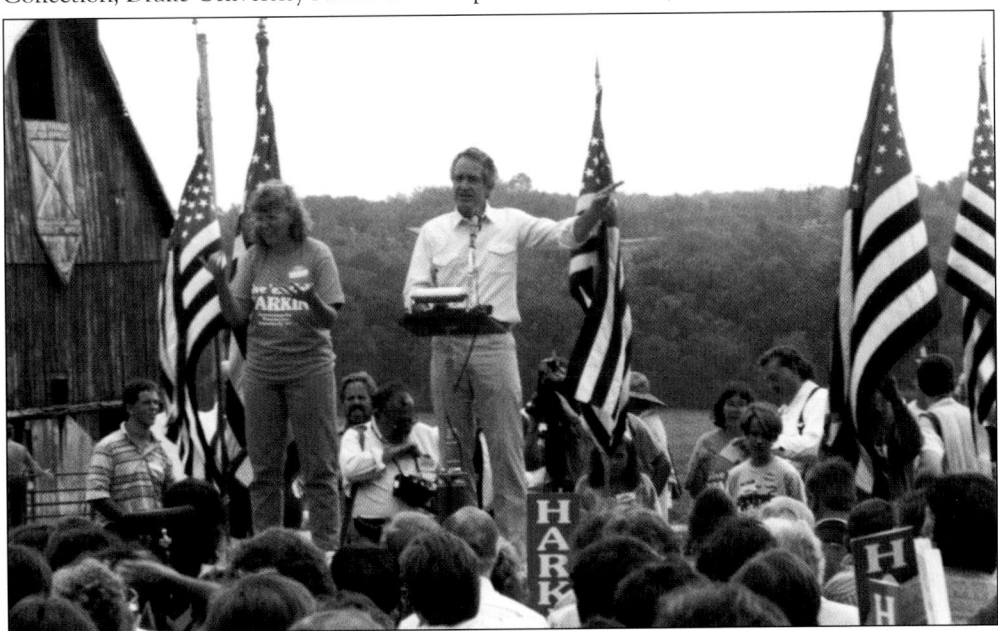

Iowa senator Tom Harkin used the 1991 Harkin Steak Fry in Winterset as a platform to announce his candidacy for president. With Harkin in the race and guaranteed a win in Iowa, other Democrats did not actively campaign. Given an incumbent Republican president, Iowa voters on both sides of the aisle had a quiet year. (Courtesy of the Harkin Collection, Drake University Archives and Special Collections.)

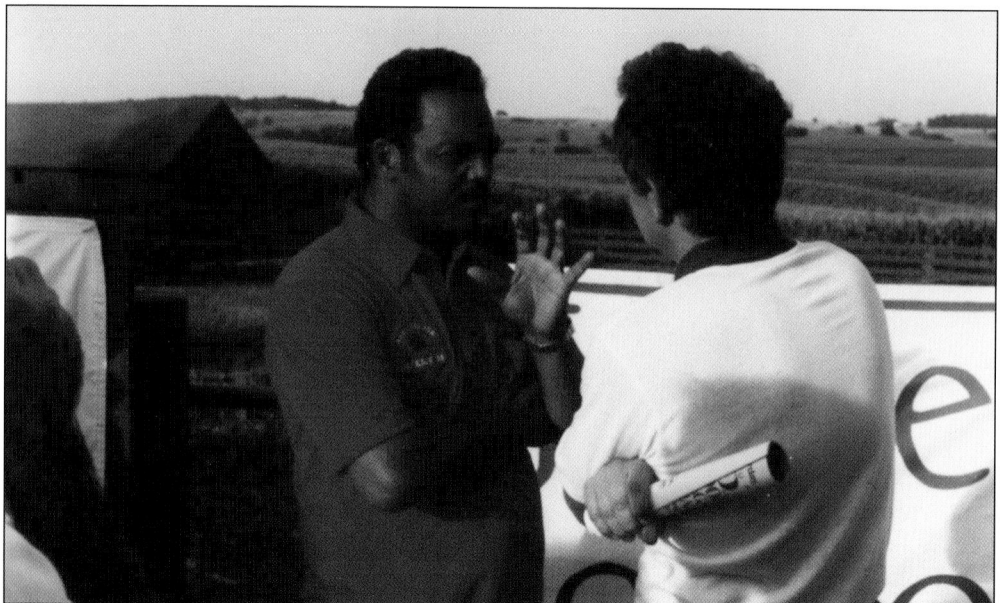

Jesse Jackson became the first African American candidate to run a competitive national presidential campaign in 1984, though he only captured two percent support among caucusgoers. Critics of the Iowa caucus continue to note that Iowa's population is predominantly white, though Jackson's campaign was very active and well received in the state. (Courtesy of the Harkin Collection, Drake University Archives and Special Collections.)

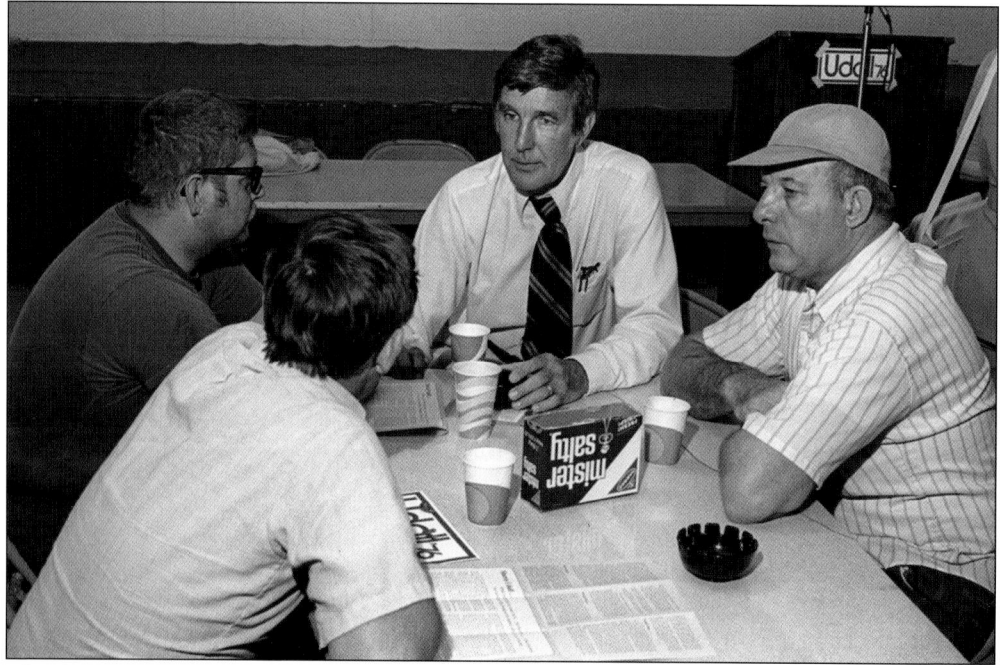

The close relationships between voters and candidates in Iowa develop during repeated interactions. Mo Udall (D-AZ), like Jimmy Carter, invested in the early Iowa campaign in 1975. On caucus night, despite erroneous reports that Udall had won, he received just one percent of the vote. Carter's 27 percent received extensive media attention. (Courtesy of Keith Wessel.)

Three

RITUALS AND CUSTOMS NEW AND OLD

Like any state, Iowa has its fair share of eccentricities. Since 1972, candidates have learned the habits of Iowa voters: coffee bean polls at the Hamburg Inn No. 2, sundaes at the Ice Cream Palace in LeMars, and pork chops on a stick. For those who would be president, Iowa offers a host of culinary treats alongside hands to shake.

Among the traditions of Iowa is the 99-county tour, a venture following in the footsteps of longtime Iowa Republican senator Chuck Grassley's annual trek. Rick Santorum, winner of the 2012 caucuses, was the first to complete the tour in 2015, reflecting on the exercise by saying, "You get a chance to sit around and talk to real people." He continued, "You meet people, and you connect with folks like we have here in Lyon County, and then you recruit other folks to be your caucus chairs, to recruit other folks to speak for you in the caucuses." Lyon County has just under 12,000 people, with approximately 8,500 registered voters.

In the year before a presidential election, candidates can be seen at Iowa staples like the Iowa State Fair, where the state's largest newspaper, the *Des Moines Register*, sets up its soapbox and allows candidates to speak for 15 minutes. It was at the 2011 soapbox that candidate Mitt Romney responded to a heckler by saying, "Corporations are people, my friend." These Iowa traditions can yield unexpected campaign spokespeople. In 2007, the Obama campaign featured a radio advertisement in which Norma "Duffy" Lyon endorsed the candidate. Duffy Lyon was known in Iowa for crafting the butter cow at the Iowa State Fair for more than 40 years—a life-sized cow made entirely of butter. (She also created butter sculptures of John Wayne, Elvis, and da Vinci's *The Last Supper.*)

But it is not just the Iowa State Fair. Candidates frequently march in community parades, participate in local celebrations, and attend fundraising events for political parties and candidates. The sun has set on two well-recognized events, the Harkin Steak Fry (Democratic, 1972–2015) and the Iowa Straw Poll (Republican, 1979–2011), but local and statewide party events continue. In 2015, newly elected US senator Joni Ernst (R-IA) created a new event, the Roast and Ride, in the tradition of the Harkin Steak Fry.

The rituals of the Iowa caucuses serve as a means to connect candidates and voters in unique ways.

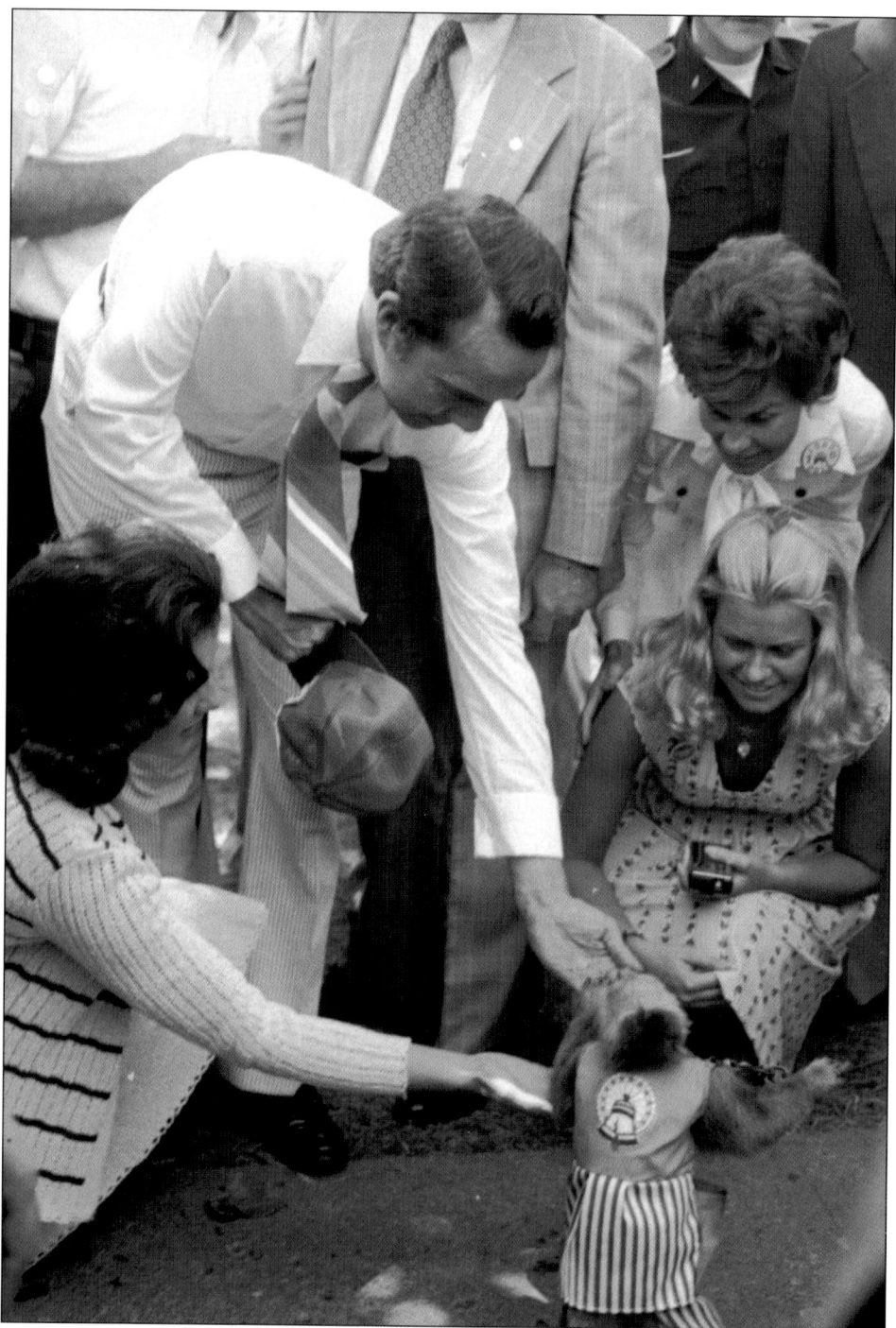

Sen. Bob Dole (R-KS) and his wife, Elizabeth, meet a monkey grinder at the Iowa State Fair in 1976, when he was President Ford's vice-presidential candidate. Dole would go on to seek and win the Republican nomination in 1996. His Midwestern roots propelled him to a first-place win over Pat Buchanan. (Courtesy of the David Penney Collection, State Historical Society of Iowa, Des Moines.)

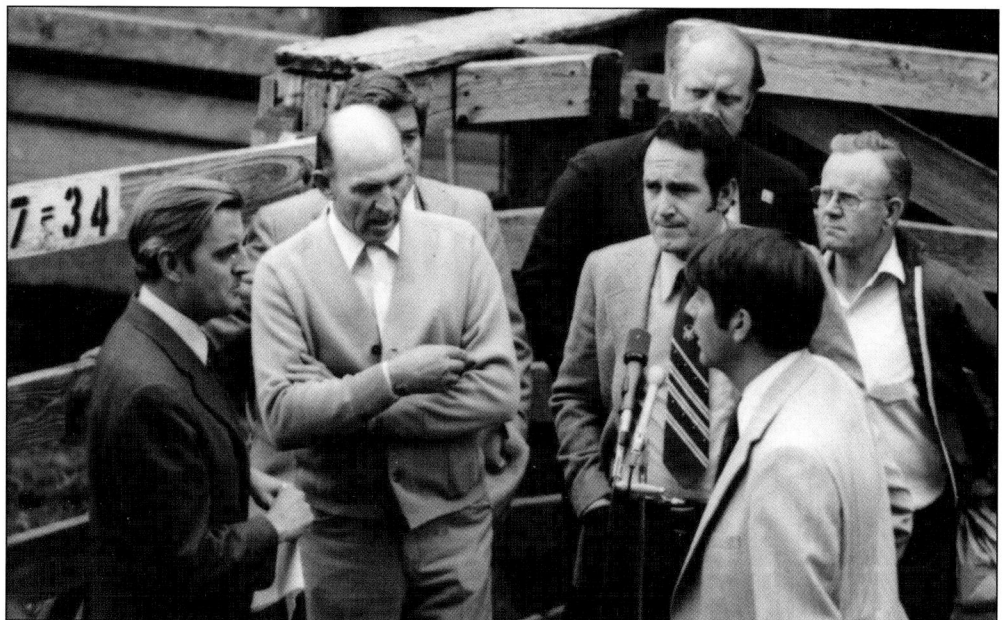

The annual Iowa State Fair attracts politicians of all stripes, many of whom seem out of place in the setting, including Vice Pres. Walter Mondale (pictured at left with his aides at the state fair), who visited in 1983. Mondale went on to a big win in the 1984 Iowa caucuses, winning 49 percent of the preference vote. (Courtesy of the Harkin Collection, Drake University Archives and Special Collections.)

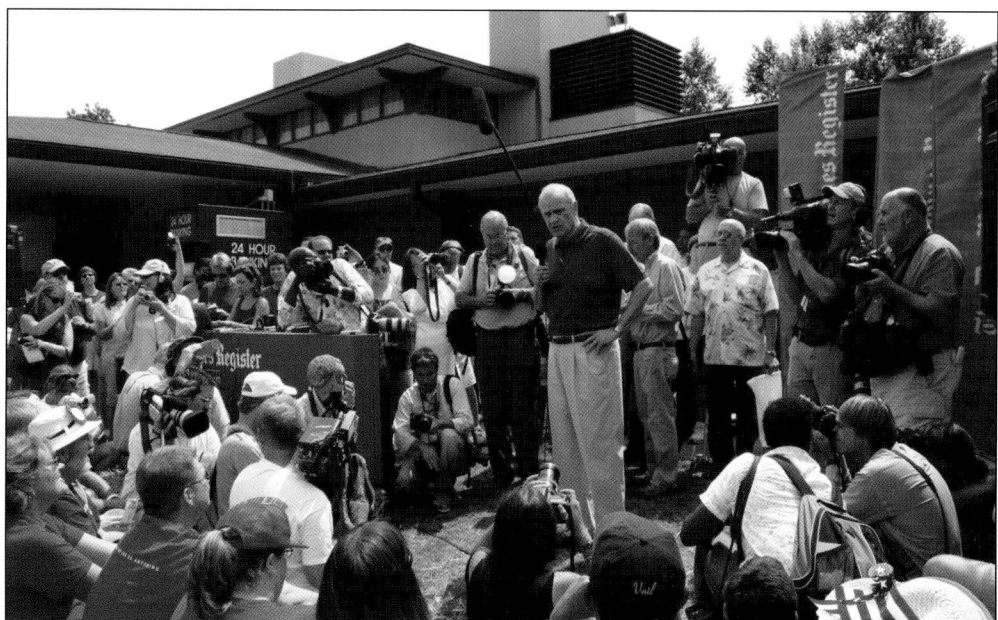

Sen. Fred Thompson (R-TN) appears at the *Des Moines Register* Soapbox at the Iowa State Fair in August 2007. Prior to announcing his candidacy for the presidency, Thompson routinely polled in the top two to three favorites during the summer of 2007. He declared his candidacy on September 5, less than four months ahead of the Iowa caucuses, and won just 13 percent of the vote among Republican caucus-goers. (Courtesy of Jordan Oster.)

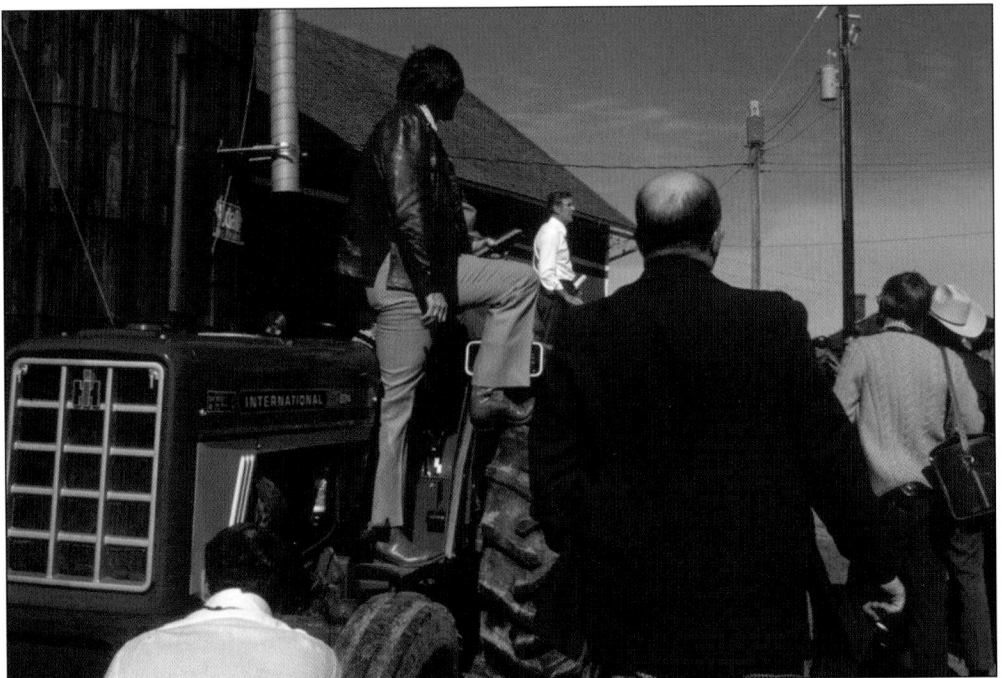

Like most candidates who run a viable campaign in Iowa, Mo Udall understood the importance of rural populations in the state. Campaigning at a farm in 1975, Udall stands outside a barn with a tractor, two unmistakable emblems of agricultural life. As an ardent environmentalist, Udall identified with independent farmers who felt a deep connection to the land. (Courtesy of Keith Wessel.)

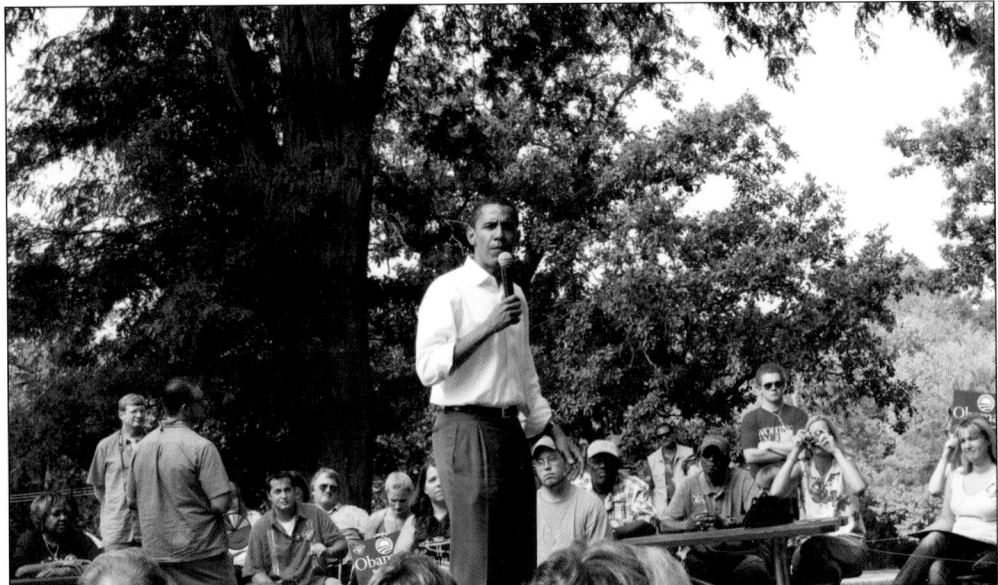

As a traditionally agricultural state with strong local communities, candidates frequently choose campaign events in local parks and town squares, often featuring picnic fare. Here, then-senator Barack Obama holds a campaign event in the spring of 2007 in Union Park, Des Moines. (Courtesy of Jordan Oster.)

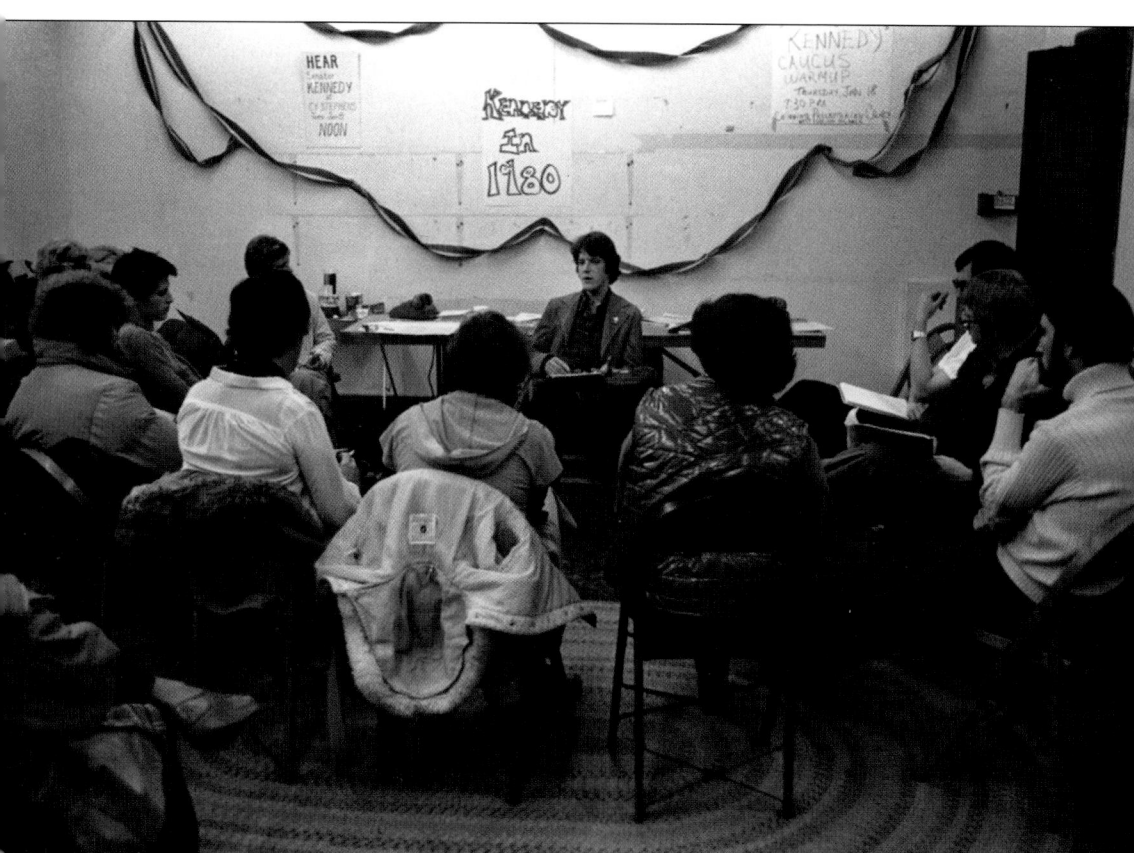

As candidates set up their initial campaign offices in Iowa, they typically rely on a small group of dedicated staff and supporters. Here, a meeting in the Kennedy campaign offices features handwritten signs, including announcements of upcoming events, one of which is called the "Kennedy Caucus Warmup." Ted Kennedy ran an unanticipated, and unsuccessful, campaign against incumbent Jimmy Carter in 1980. (Courtesy of Keith Wessel.)

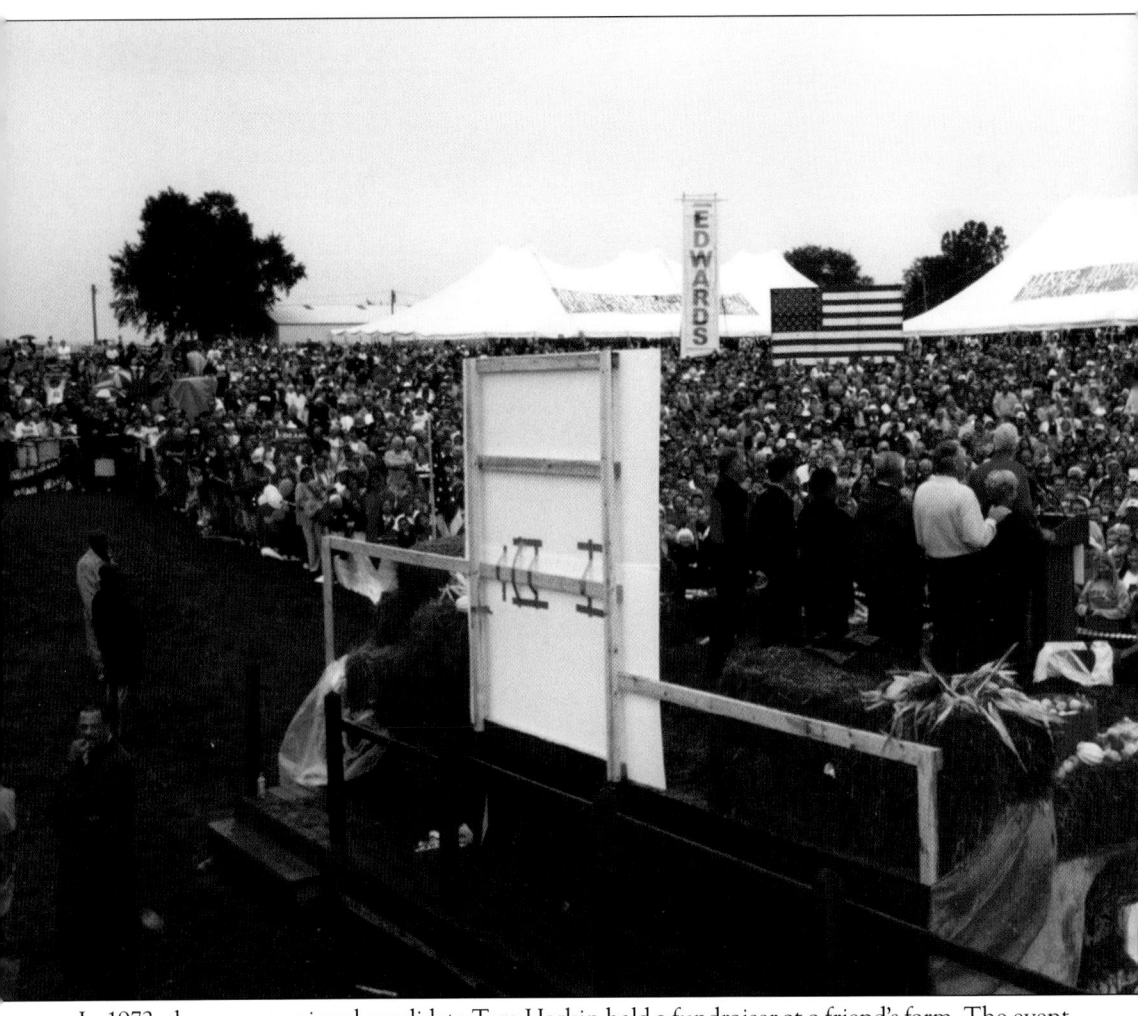

In 1972, then-congressional candidate Tom Harkin held a fundraiser at a friend's farm. The event turned into an annual Democratic ritual, the Harkin Steak Fry, attracting national politicos and elected officials until Harkin's retirement from the US Senate in 2015. It was moved to the Indianola Balloon Field (home of the National Balloon Classic every summer) and became a

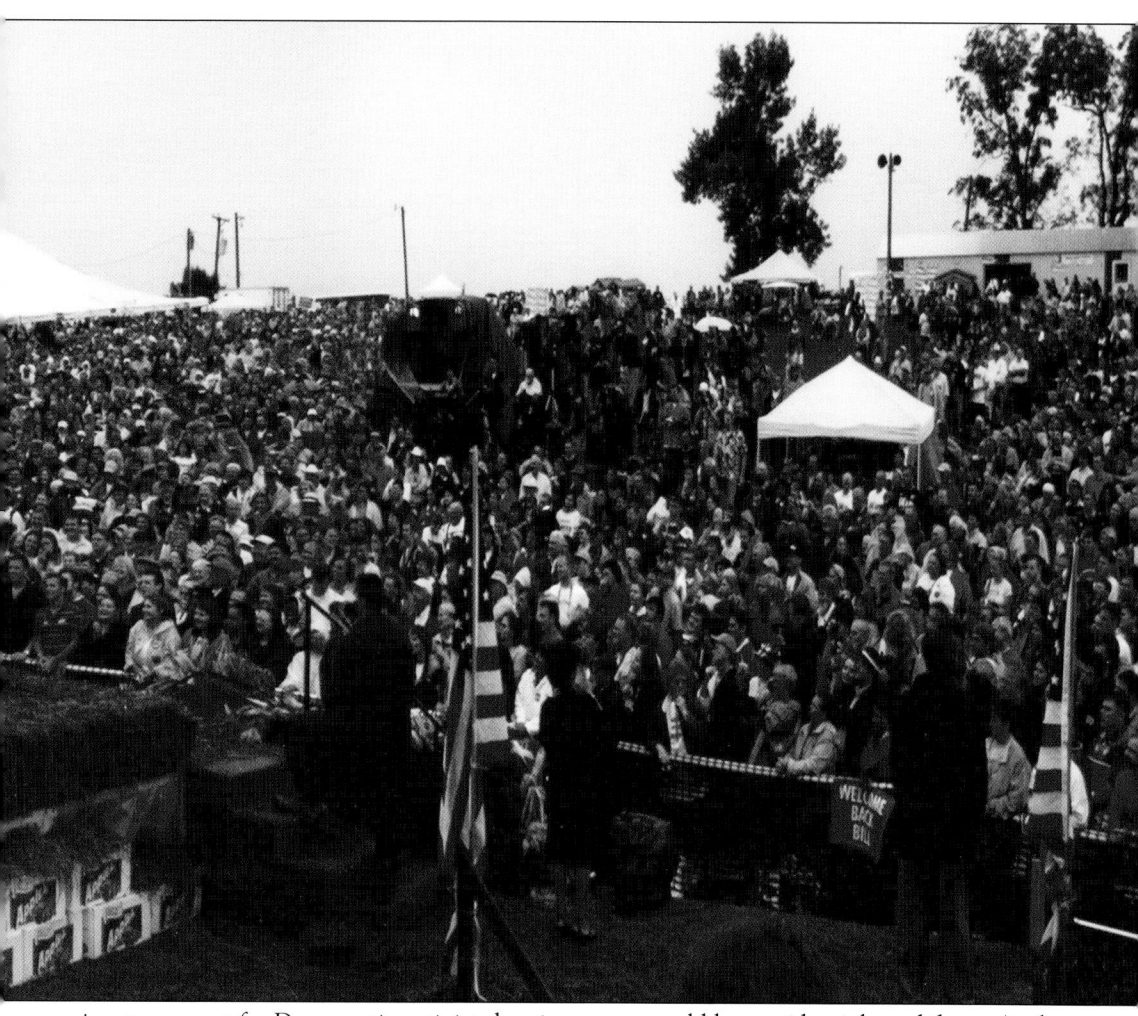

signature event for Democratic activists hosting many would-be presidential candidates. At the first steak fry, tickets cost $2, and approximately 40 people attended the event. (Courtesy of the Harkin Collection, Drake University Archives and Special Collections.)

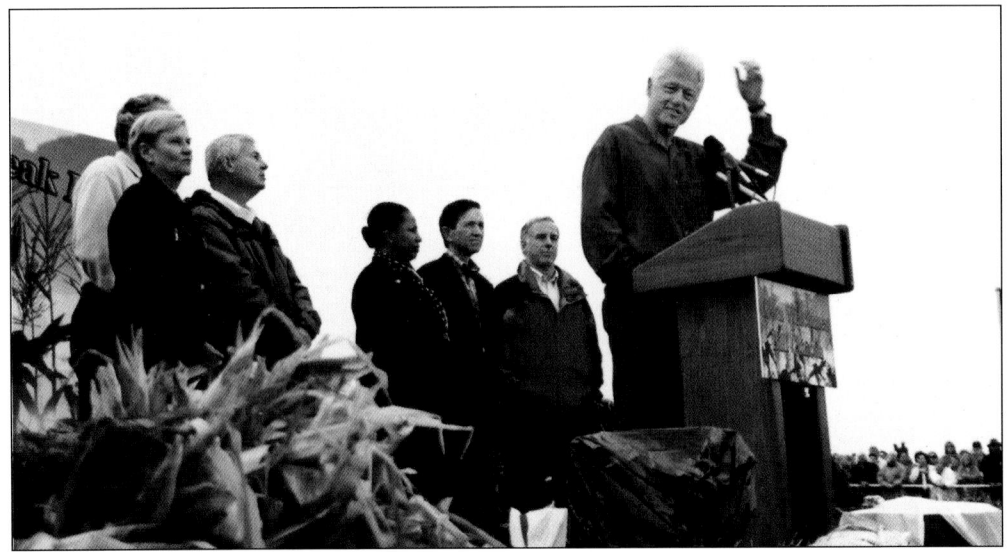

In the fall before a presidential caucus, the steak fry would typically offer a chance for all of the candidates seeking the nomination to speak to the crowd. In 2003, the event featured former president Bill Clinton, with presidential candidates Carol Moseley Braun (center), Dennis Kucinich (second from right), and Howard Dean (far right). (Courtesy of the Harkin Collection, Drake University Archives and Special Collections.)

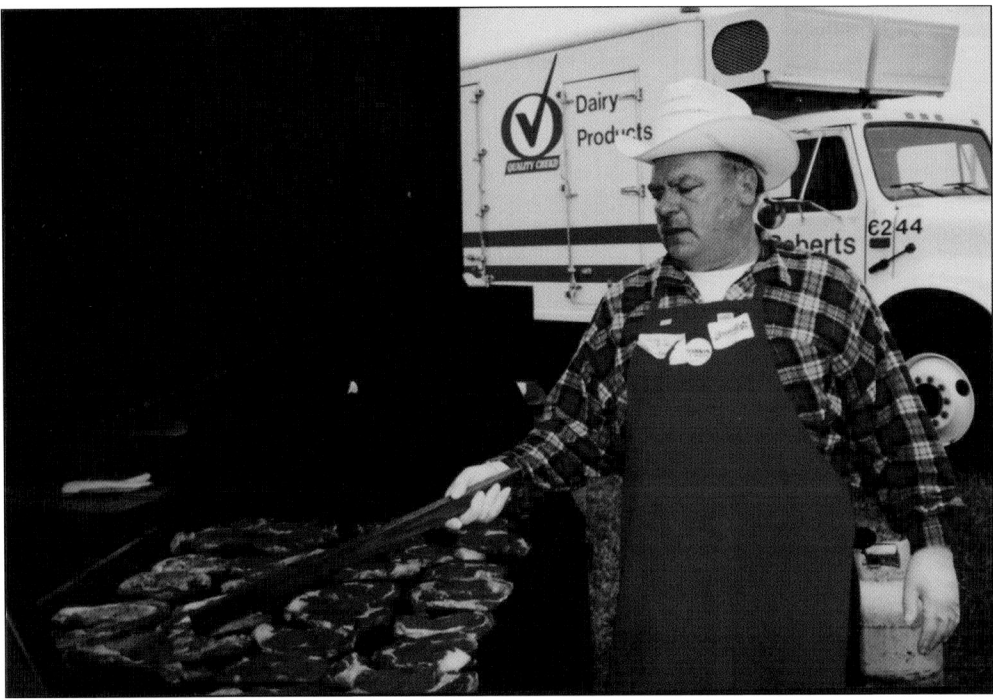

As its name suggests, a ticket to the Harkin Steak Fry included a steak. Although Iowa is well known for hog production, few realize that the state has (as of this writing) nearly 28,000 cattle operations and ranks seventh in the United States in beef production. At the final Harkin Steak Fry 2015, attendance was estimated at 10,000 based on the number of steaks served. (Courtesy of the Harkin Collection, Drake University Archives and Special Collections.)

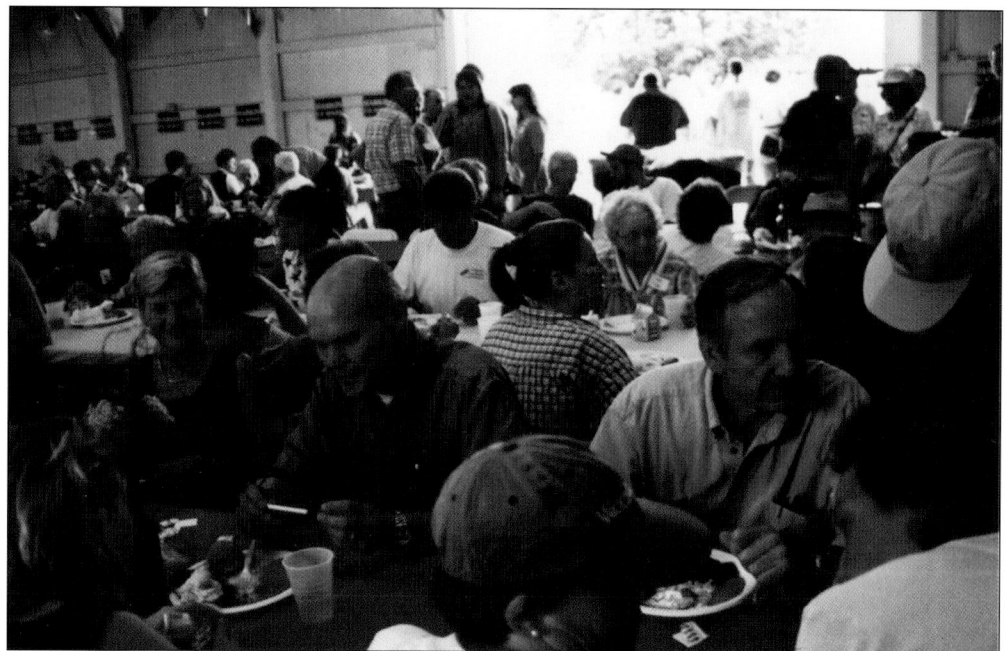

The Harkin Steak Fry (1972–2015) was an outdoor event, with attendees enjoying grilled steak. Pictured here in 1998 is Democratic political figure James Carville (dark-blue shirt), who had gained notoriety as an architect of Bill Clinton's successful 1992 presidential campaign and returned as the featured speaker. Clinton had competed against Tom Harkin (light-blue shirt) for the 1992 Democratic nomination. (Courtesy of the Harkin Collection, Drake University Archives and Special Collections.)

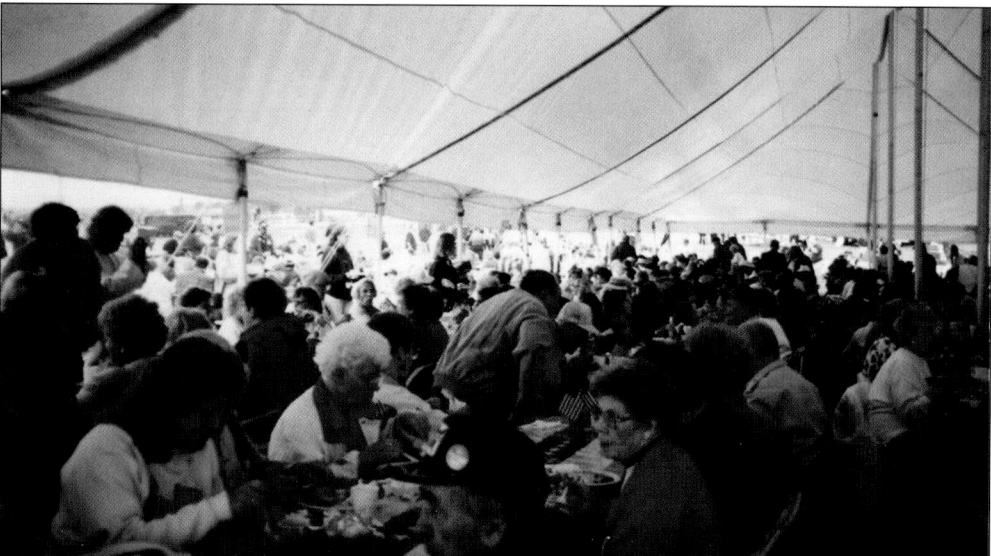

Although speakers at the Harkin Steak Fry would appear at an uncovered stage, attendees had a chance to move under the tent to enjoy their meal, which was particularly welcome during some cold, muddy Iowa fall days. Candidates and those considering a run for the presidency would stroll through the crowd, shaking hands and talking policy. (Courtesy of the Harkin Collection, Drake University Archives and Special Collections.)

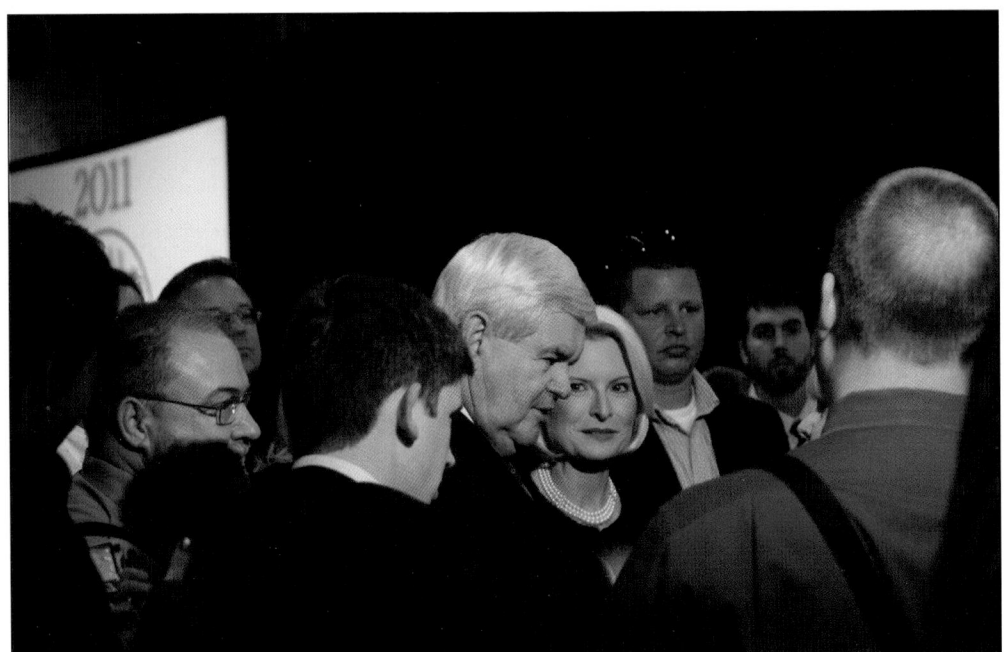

The Iowa Republican Party holds its annual Reagan Dinner each year, though the year before a caucus yields the highest attendance. The event is a fundraiser for the party but also provides a platform for presidential candidates to speak to the party faithful. The 2011 dinner included five candidates. Both Newt Gingrich (above, with wife, Callista) and Rick Santorum (below) were well received by the crowd. Gingrich was often at the top of the polls during the fall of 2011, but Santorum surged in the final weeks of the campaign. Gingrich came in fourth, while Santorum narrowly bested Mitt Romney. (Both author's collection.)

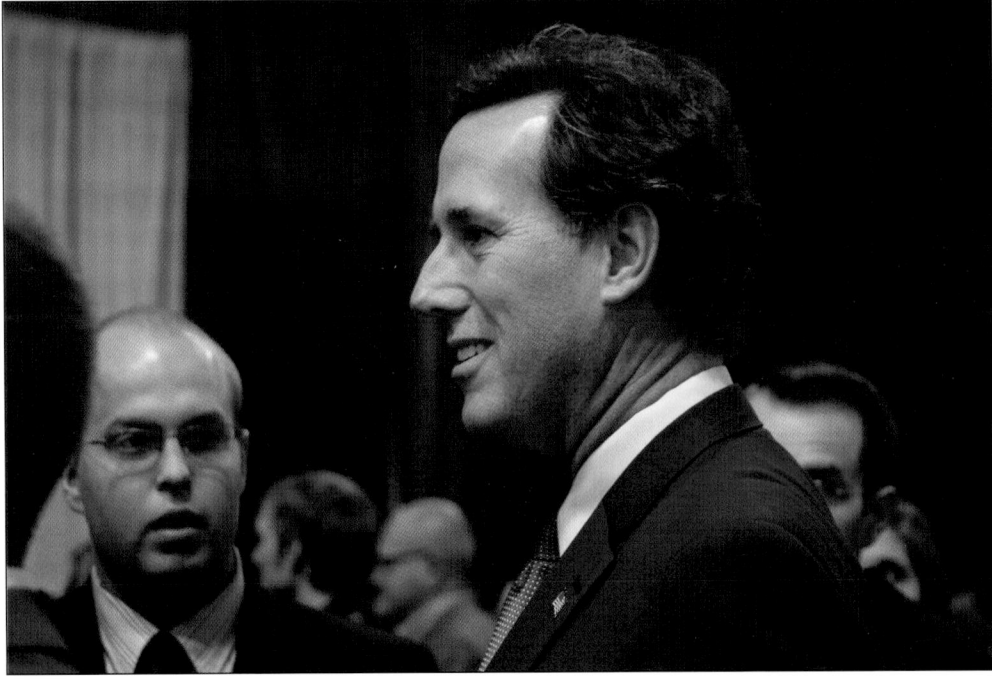

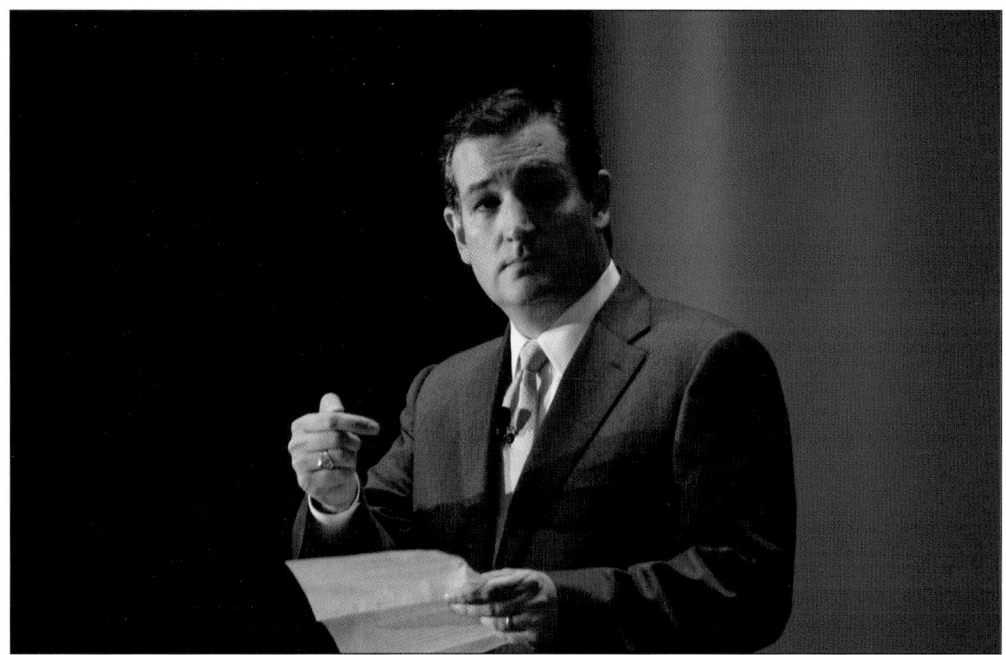

The 2013 GOP Reagan Dinner featured Texas senator Ted Cruz, pictured above, who went on to declare his intention to run for president in March 2015. Earlier that fall, Cruz had made a name for himself among Republicans nationwide when he spoke for more than 20 hours about the need to defund Obamacare. In addition to the Reagan dinner, the state GOP organization holds the annual Lincoln Dinner. In 2014, the dinner featured former vice-presidential candidate Rep. Paul Ryan (R-WI), pictured below, who is widely considered a potential presidential contender in coming years. (Above, author's collection; below, courtesy of the Republican Party of Iowa.)

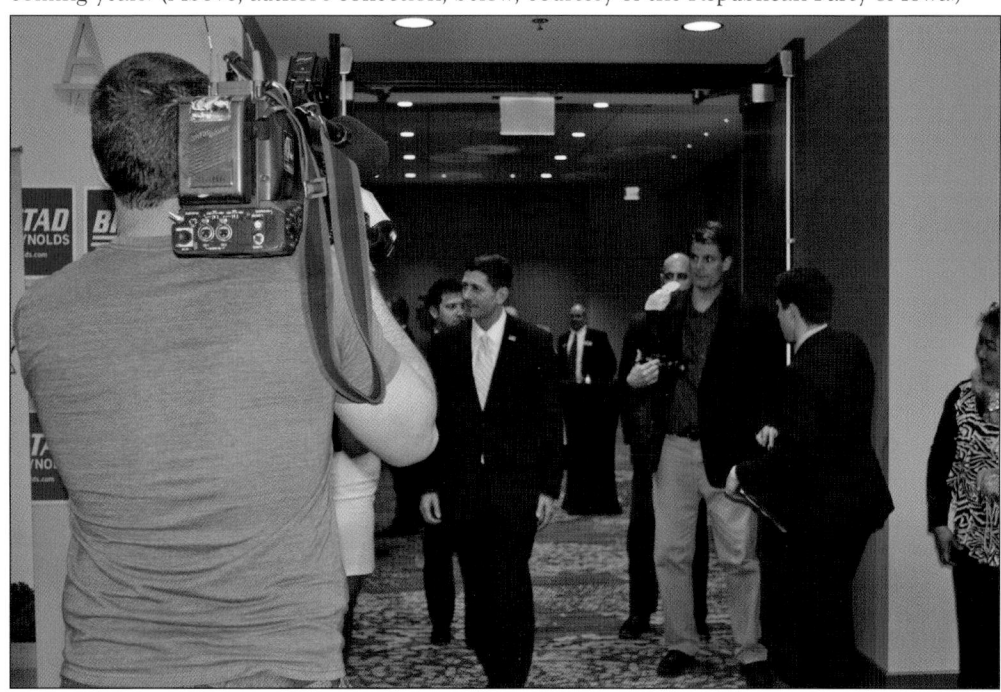

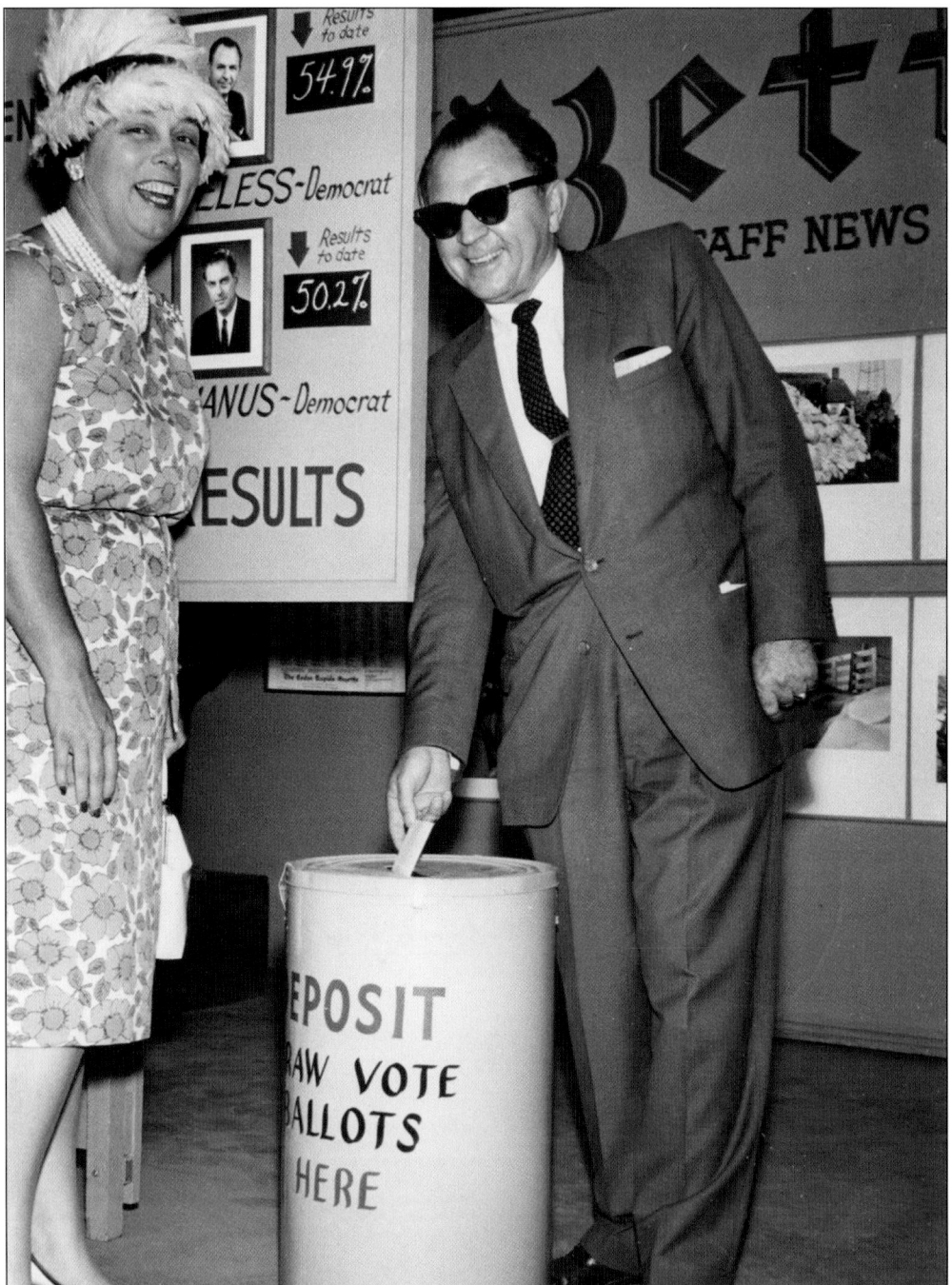

From 1979 until 2011, the Republican Party of Iowa held the Iowa Straw Poll in Ames. But the tradition of straw polls at community events around the state has had a long history, as seen in this 1962 photograph. Straw polls, or informal preference votes, were often sponsored by local newspapers. (Courtesy of Frank Nye Papers, University of Iowa Libraries, Iowa City, Iowa.)

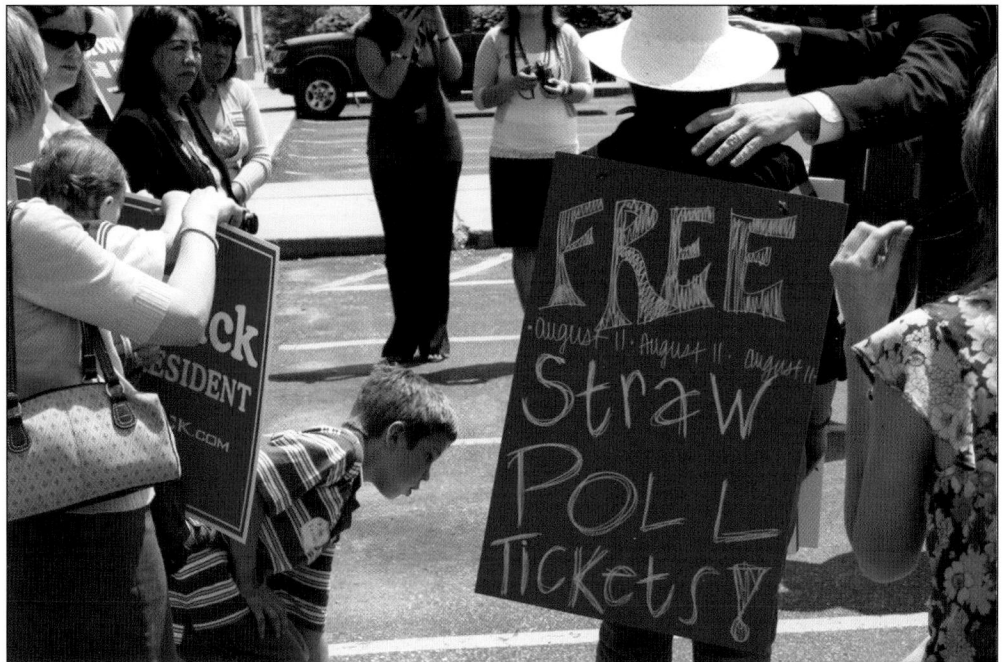

The Iowa Straw Poll gave Republican activists an opportunity to cast an early vote for their favored candidate. Campaigns would buy tickets to offer supporters in the hopes of winning the contest and gaining momentum on the campaign trail as the Brownback campaign did in 2011 (pictured). As a result, the event was widely seen by analysts as a good test of a campaign's organizational prowess in advance of the caucuses. (Courtesy of Jordan Oster.)

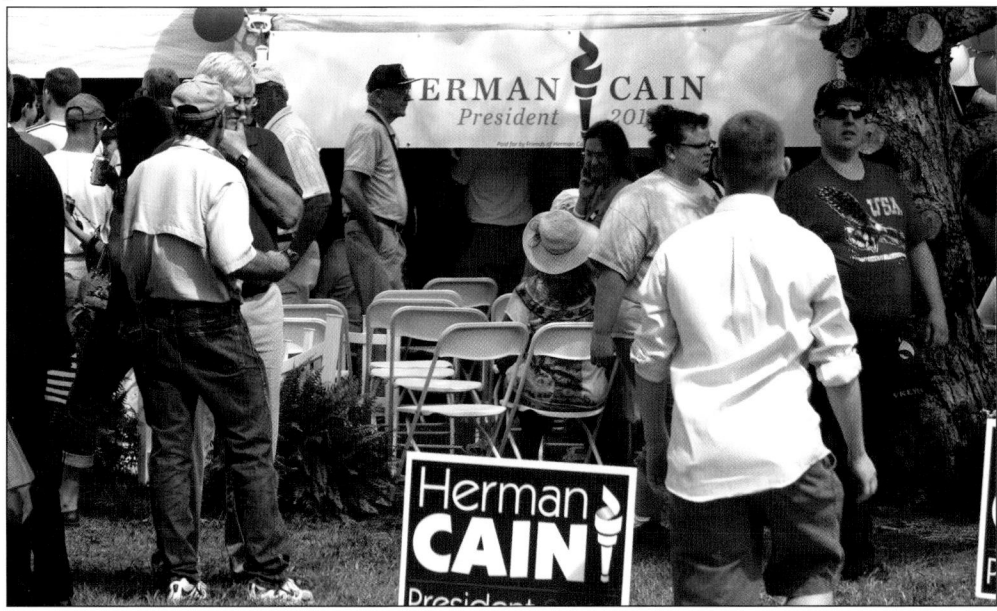

From 1979 until 2011, the Republican Party of Iowa held a late-summer fundraiser, the Iowa Straw Poll. Candidates would bid for space and set up tents, like this one by the Herman Cain camp in 2012. Appropriately, the tent featured Godfather's pizza (Cain was the chief executive officer of Godfather's), while a gospel choir provided entertainment. (Author's collection.)

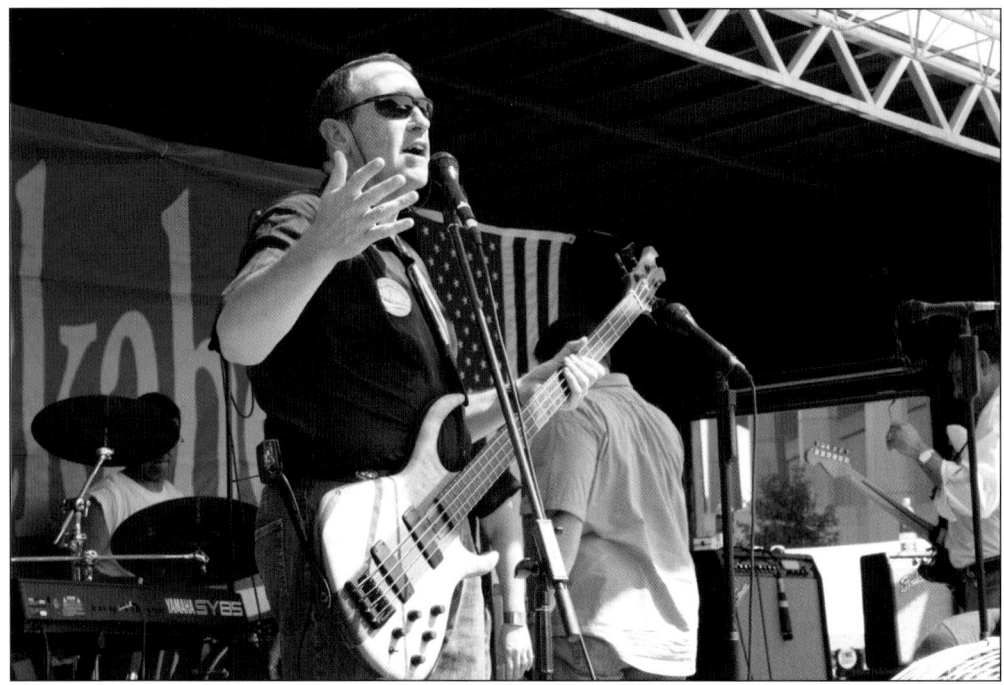

The Iowa Straw Poll (frequently called the Ames Straw Poll because it was always held on the campus of Iowa State University in Ames, Iowa) was a feature of Republican presidential campaigns until 2011. In 2007, Mike Huckabee's space featured fresh Arkansas watermelon and live band performances with Huckabee playing bass. (Courtesy of Jordan Oster.)

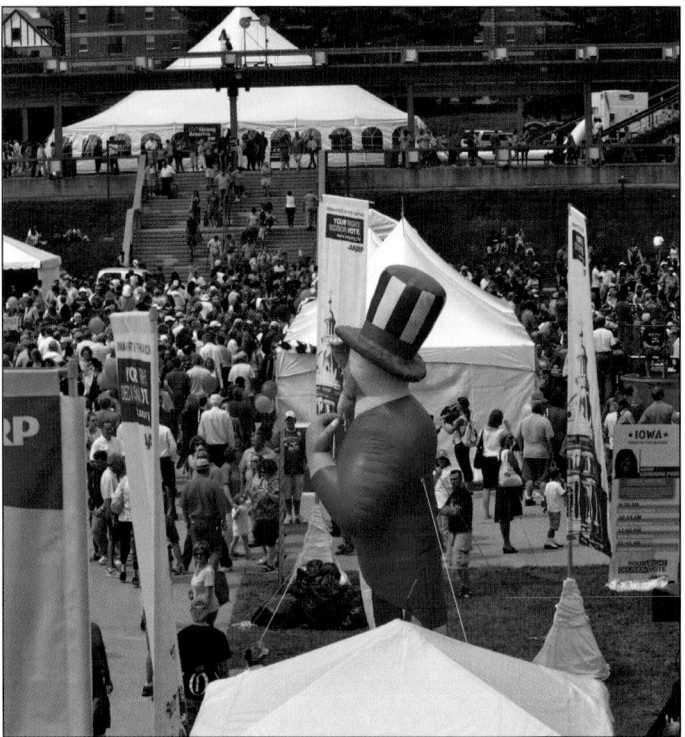

The Iowa Straw Poll (or Ames Straw Poll) is a fundraising event held by the Republican Party of Iowa the August before a presidential caucus in which party activists participate in a preference vote. Candidates bid on locations on the campus of Iowa State University. In 2011, Ron Paul won the coveted position just outside the polling location; nonetheless, the Bachmann campaign bested Paul by about 150 votes. (Author's collection.)

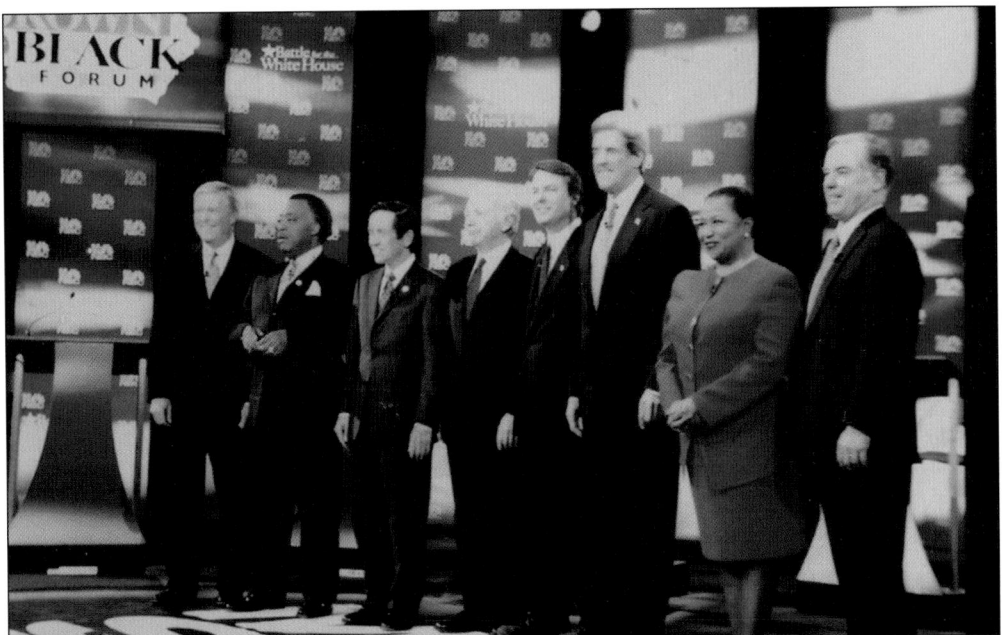

In 1980, Des Moines activists Wayne Ford and Mary Campos invited candidates to attend a forum devoted to issues of concern to minority communities. It turned into a regular event, the Brown and Black Forum, for Democratic candidates. In 2015, the Republican Party of Iowa announced that it would partner with Urban Dreams for the first Republican Brown and Black Forum, though the event was later cancelled due to scheduling issues. The forum is one of the longest-running candidate events and the only event that focuses attention on minority voters. Here, the Democratic candidates take the stage in 2003. (Courtesy of Urban Dreams.)

The Hamburg Inn No. 2, a family diner in Iowa City, has hosted several presidential candidates, including Ronald Reagan, Pat Buchanan, Howard Dean, Wesley Clark, Barack Obama, and Dennis Kucinich. During the fall before a caucus, guests at the "Burg" receive a coffee bean to place in the jar of their preferred candidate. The coffee bean poll was featured in an episode of *The West Wing* as one of the rituals of the Iowa campaign trail. (Author's collection.)

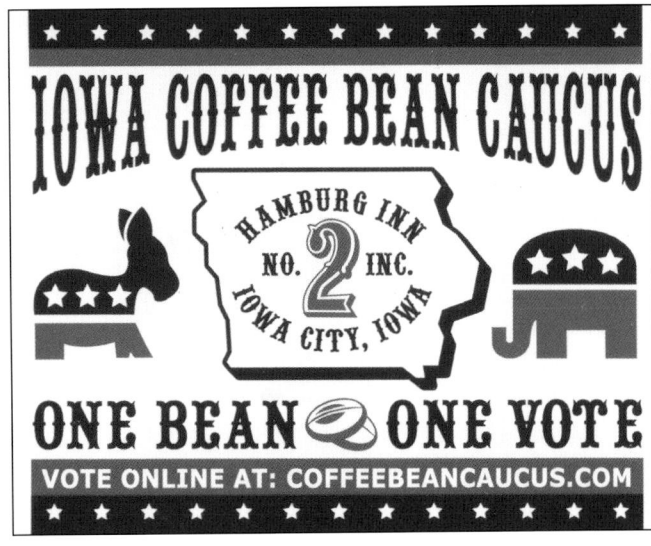

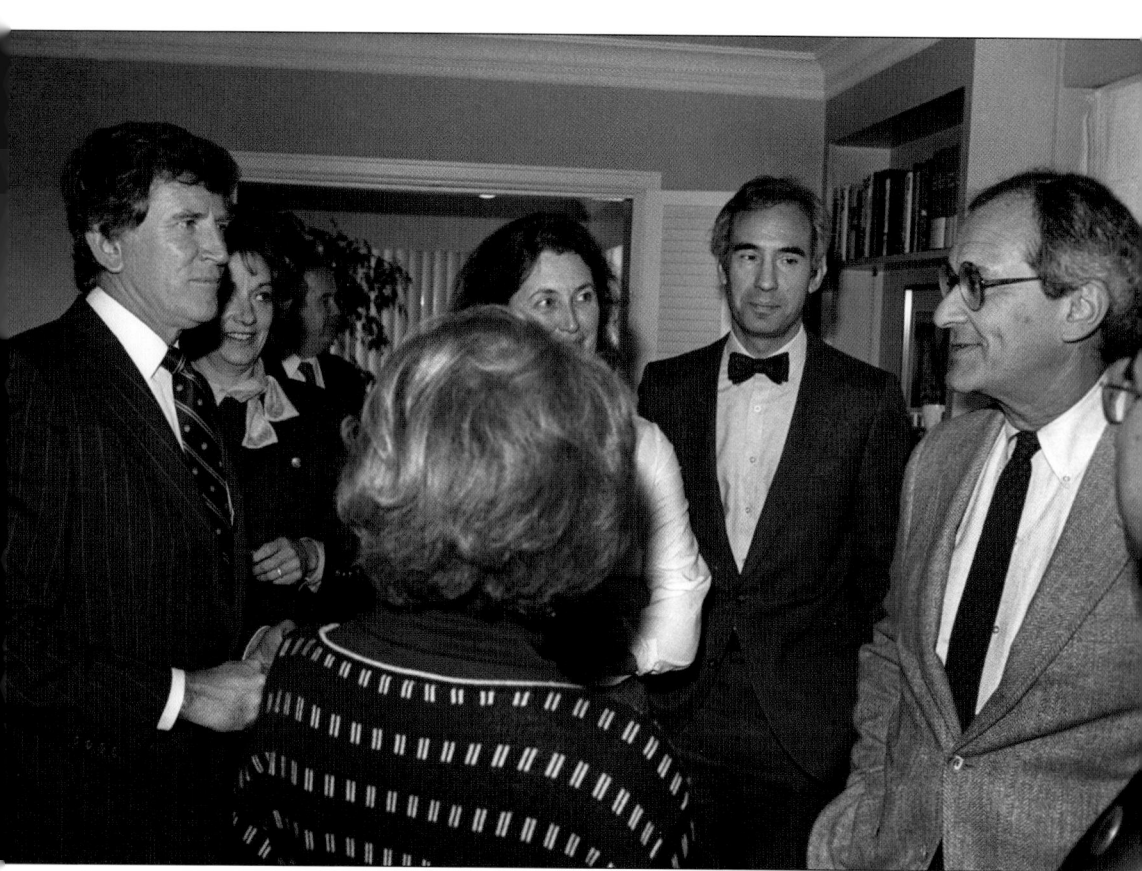

House parties give candidates an opportunity to interact with party activists in an intimate setting, like this one with Gary Hart in 1987. Hart suspended his campaign in May 1987 after it was exposed that he was having an affair. The swift demise of his campaign has come to exemplify the ways that the media has grown in power and significance. (Courtesy of Keith Wessel.)

Four

Media Is Here, There, and Everywhere

Over the past four decades, the Iowa caucuses have become an established feature of the race for the presidency. The results of the Iowa precinct caucuses, announced on caucus night every four years, are taken as a barometer of candidate success and frequently shape the dynamic of the nomination campaign. Together, Iowa and New Hampshire receive as much media attention as all other state contests combined. But the precinct caucuses are only the first step in a long process of determining state delegates to the national party conventions. Delegates elected in precinct caucuses will go on to attend county conventions; delegates elected at county conventions will go on to attend district conventions; delegates elected at district conventions will go on to attend state party conventions; and delegates elected at state party conventions will go on to attend the national party conventions. During that process, which is managed differently in the two parties, a lot can change.

Nonetheless, media attention to the Iowa caucuses has grown exponentially. In his famous book *The Making of the President 1972*, Theodore White does not have a single mention of the Iowa caucuses. Today's media outlets, in contrast, are known to embed reporters in Iowa the same way they do for overseas military units during armed conflict. National Public Radio's Don Gonyea is well recognized on the RAGBRAI (the Register's Annual Great Bicycle Ride Across Iowa) circuit. One embedded reporter, Trip Gabriel of the *New York Times*, wrote in 2015, "Iowans take their role in the presidential process very seriously. They follow the news, read policy statements and famously expect to meet candidates two or three times before making up their minds. It is my impression that they mistrust the news media a little less than elsewhere and earnestly share their views with reporters." Indeed, average Iowans are frequently asked to contribute their opinions about candidates to national media outlets.

While some reporters spend a good deal of time getting to know the state, many more spend limited time on the ground in Iowa. Media representations often rely on clichéd understandings of the state rather than a deep appreciation of the people and places that define the Iowa campaign. A Des Moines apparel company created a line of products specifically for visiting reporters in 2015. One shirt read: "Is there a bale of hay I can interview you next to?"

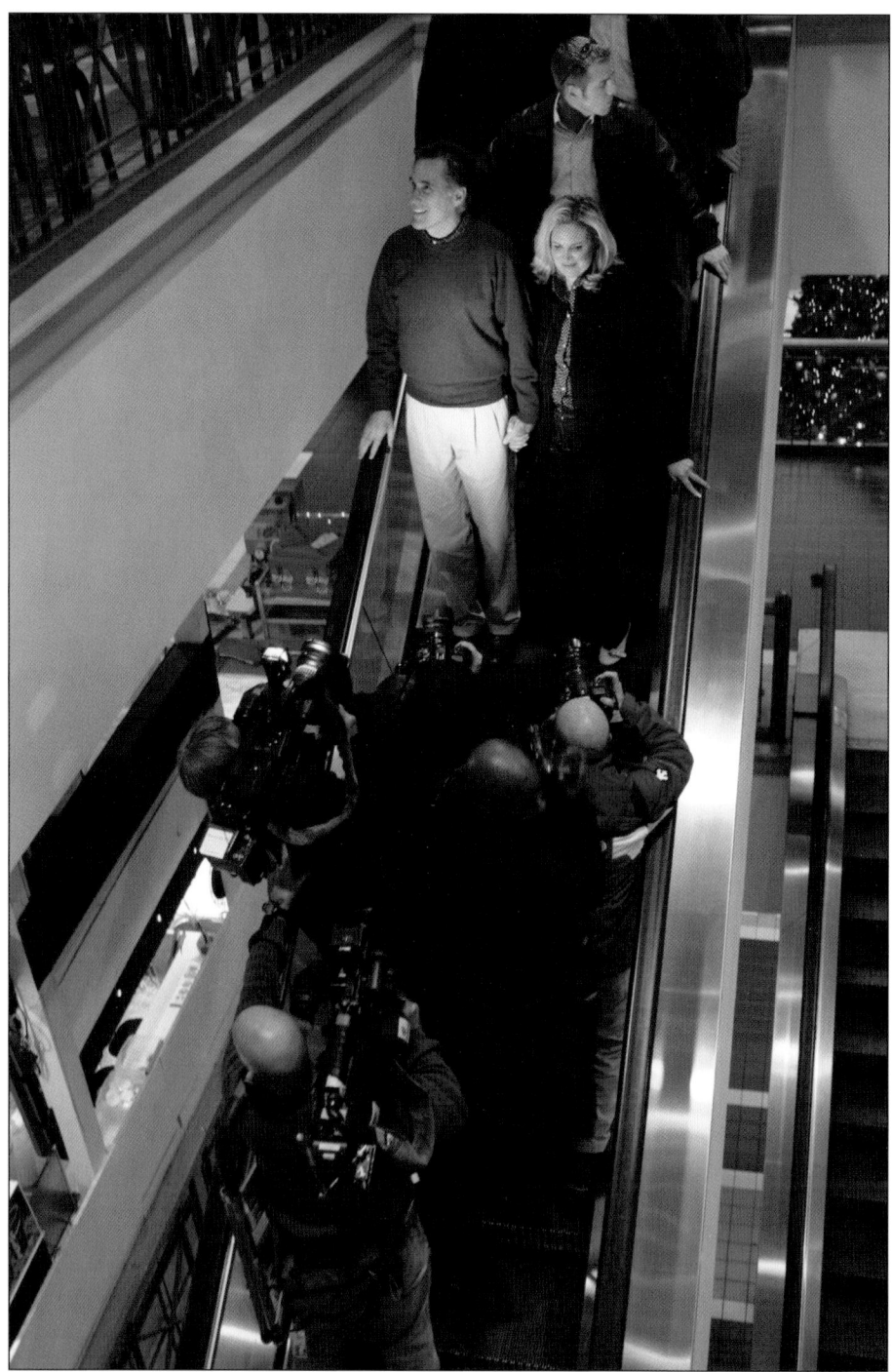

Mitt Romney and his wife, Ann, visit a shopping mall in 2011, with media documenting their escalator descent. As a front-runner candidate, media from all over the country came to Iowa to track the Romney campaign in the weeks before the caucuses. Although Romney was a national frontrunner, it was Rick Santorum who won the caucuses—besting Romney by eight votes. (Courtesy of Jordan Oster.)

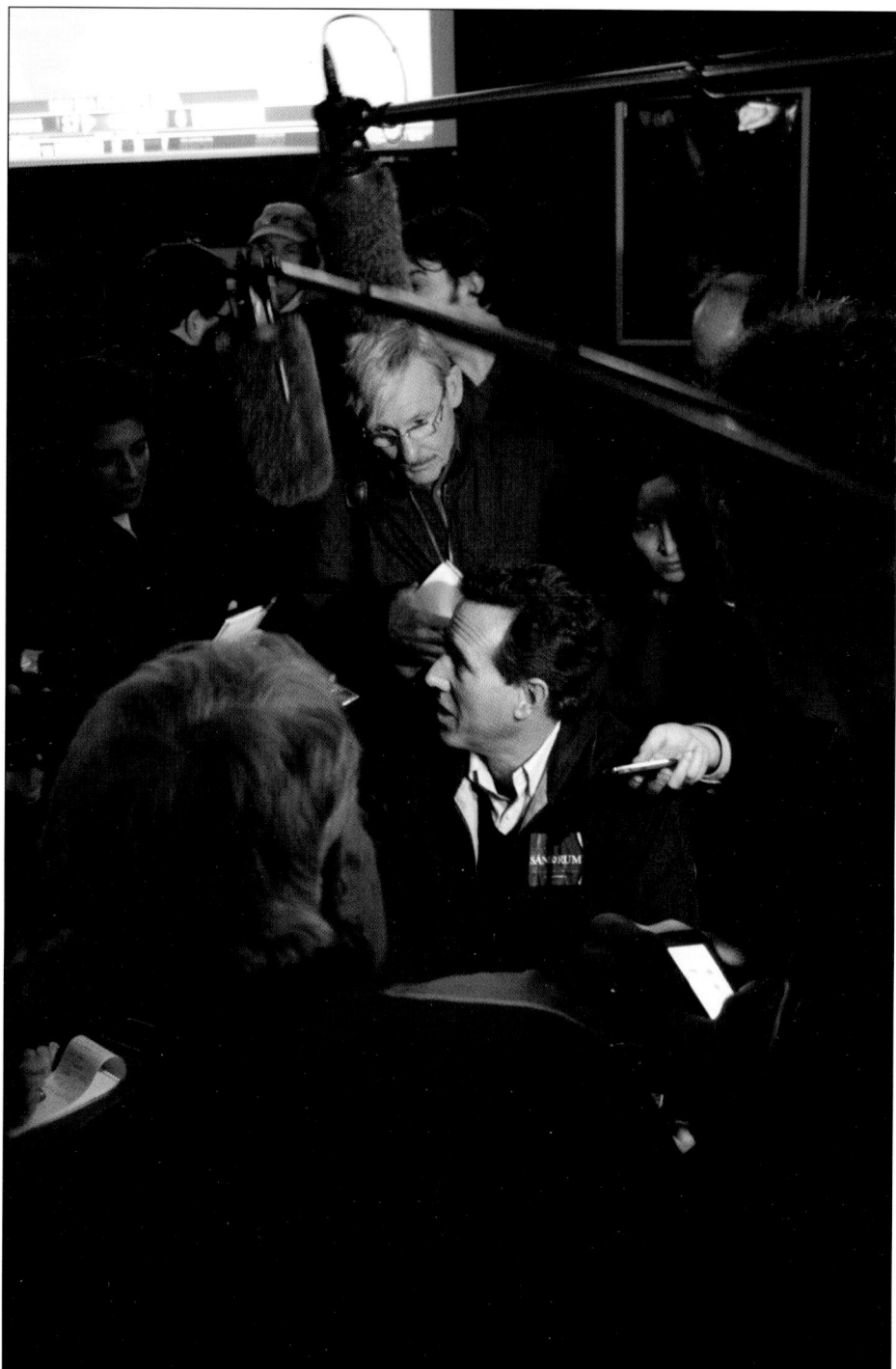

Media representatives gather around a table at a Buffalo Wild Wings in Ames, Iowa, where Rick Santorum held an event in 2012, just days before the caucuses. As the caucuses near, small events at local restaurants, businesses, and community centers frequently become overrun by reporters and cameras. (Author's collection.)

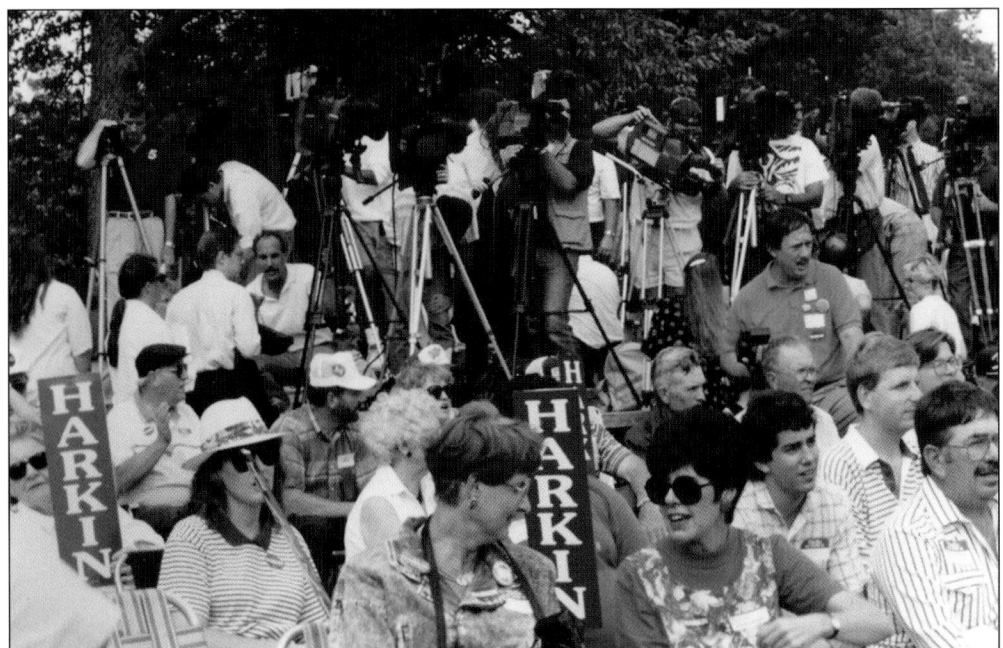

The Harkin Steak Fry, an annual fundraiser for Iowa senator Tom Harkin, regularly drew national political figures, including presidential candidates and would-be candidates to a balloon field south of Des Moines. Alongside the crowd, national media would swarm the event each year. (Courtesy of the Harkin Collection, Drake University Archives and Special Collections.)

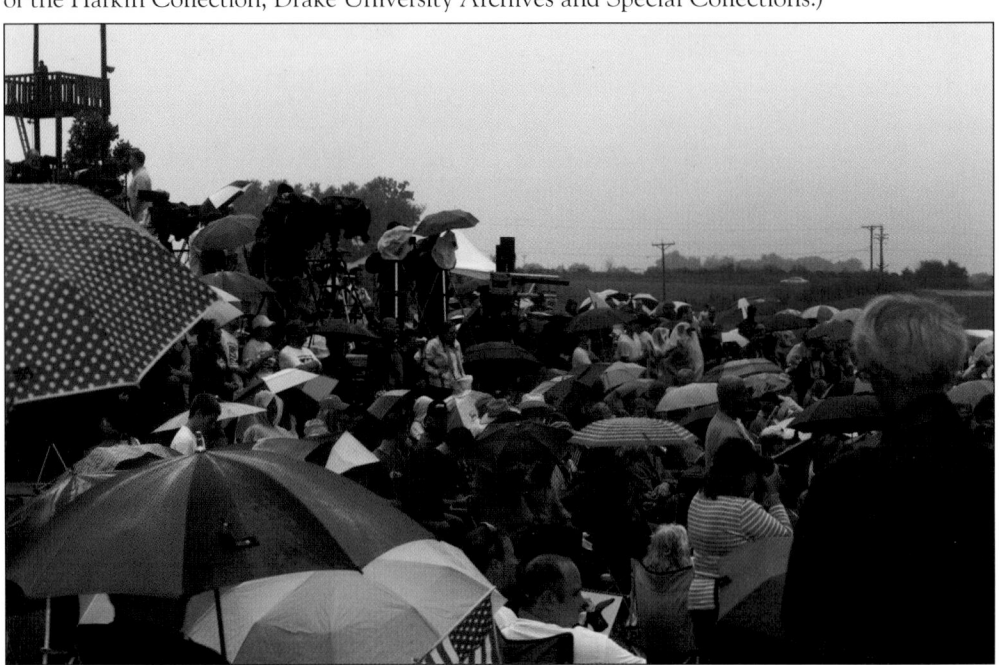

Events happen rain or shine, and this Tea Party rally in Indianola was a rainy day; nonetheless, the media was out in full force, with cameras covered by plastic bags, tarps, or umbrellas. The headliner for this event was Sarah Palin, fresh off the 2008 campaign trail as the running mate of Republican John McCain. (Author's collection.)

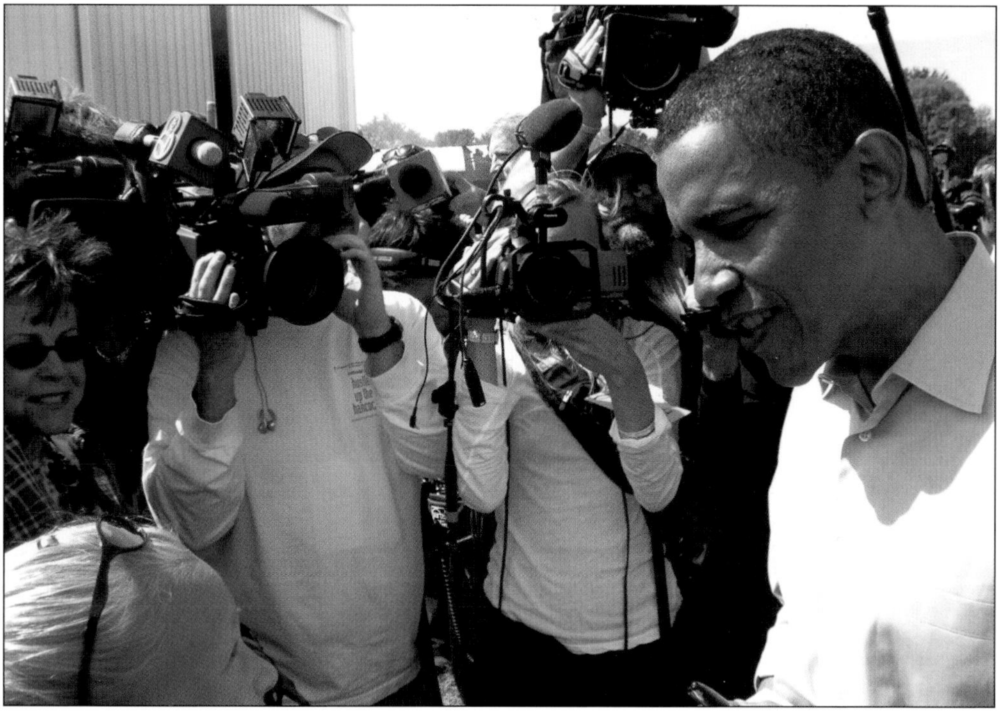

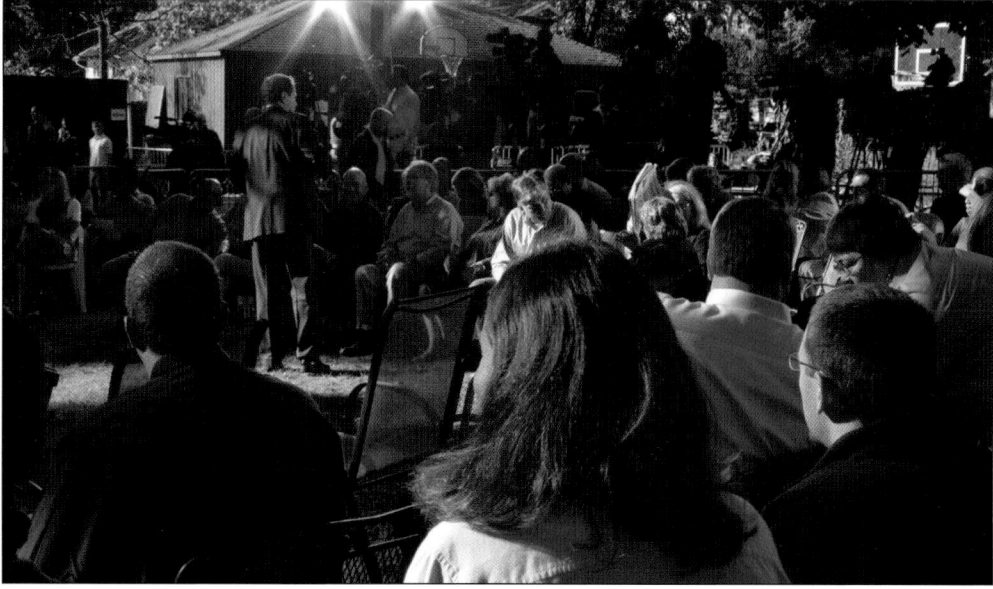

After his speech to the 2004 Democratic National Convention, first-term senator Barack Obama was the featured speaker at the 2006 Harkin Steak Fry, and national media was anxious to record the visit to the first-in-the-nation caucus state despite the fact that Obama's announcement that he would seek the presidency was still more than a year away. (Courtesy of Jordan Oster.)

In September 2010, Pres. Barack Obama returned to Iowa for a backyard chat at the home of Sandy Hatfield Clubb in the Beaverdale neighborhood of Des Moines. Nearly two years after his initial election, and more than two years before he would win reelection, Obama's visit attracted media from across the country. (Author's collection.)

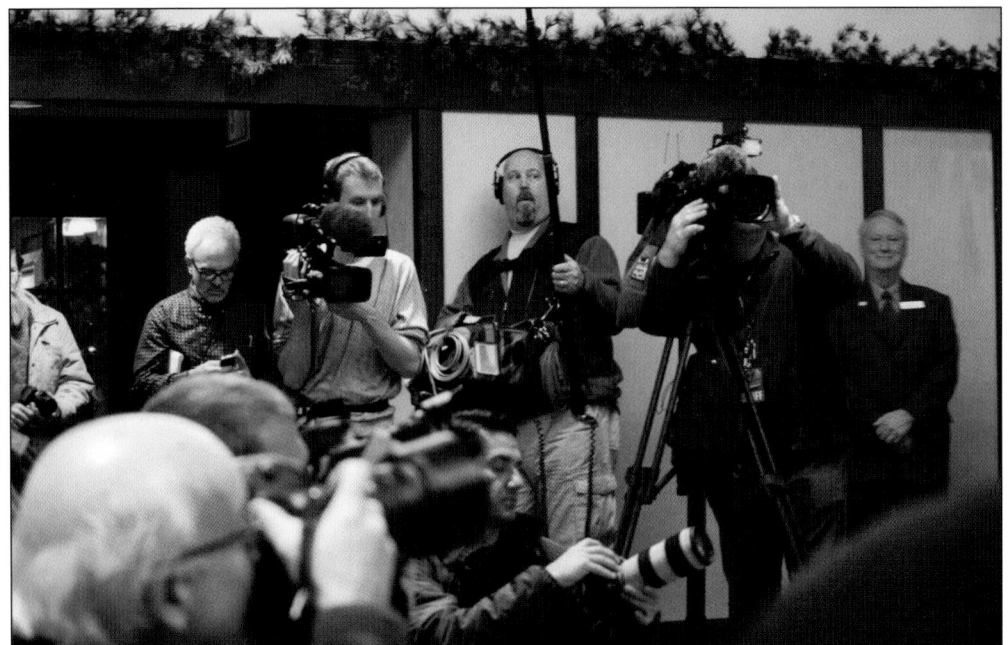

In the final days before the 2012 caucus, Ron Paul visited Perry, Iowa, for a post-Christmas visit. National media personalities, including NBC's Chuck Todd, were on hand to document Paul's final days on the campaign trail. Although Paul did not win the presidential preference vote, he did garner more delegates than any other candidate in the 2012 caucus. (Author's collection.)

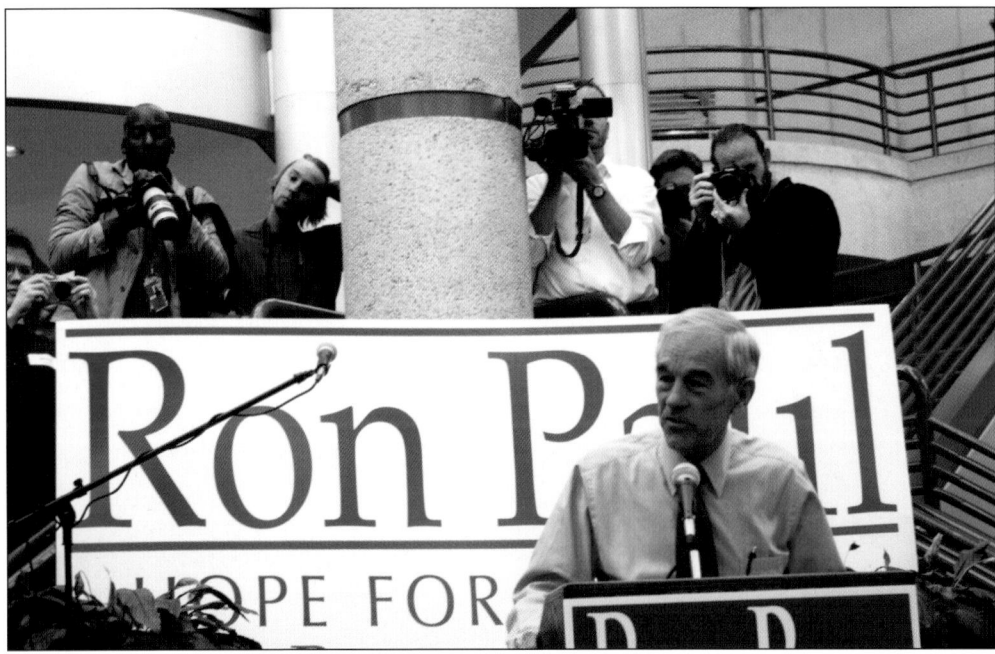

Iowa crowds are accustomed to the national media presence that follows candidates across the state. Often, reporters are more numerous and more prominent than campaign staff, as they are at this Ron Paul event in downtown Des Moines. Paul's grassroots campaign yielded more delegates on caucus night than either Rick Santorum or Mitt Romney. (Courtesy of Jordan Oster.)

In between caucus cycles, potential candidates come to Iowa to begin the process of meeting with party leaders, county party chairs, grassroots activists, consultants, and fundraisers. Local newscasters are often on the scene to document their visit, as they were for Sen. Evan Bayh (D-IN) when he visited the state in 2005, three years before the 2008 caucuses. (Courtesy of Jordan Oster.)

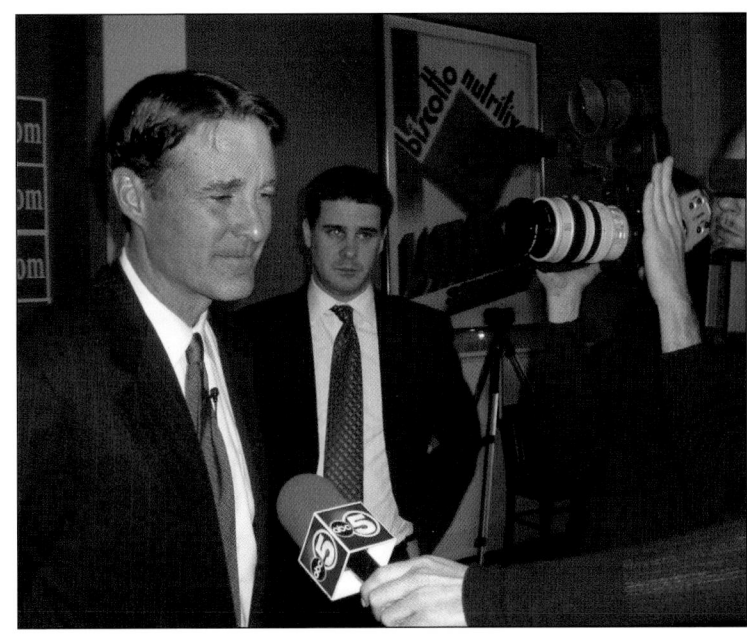

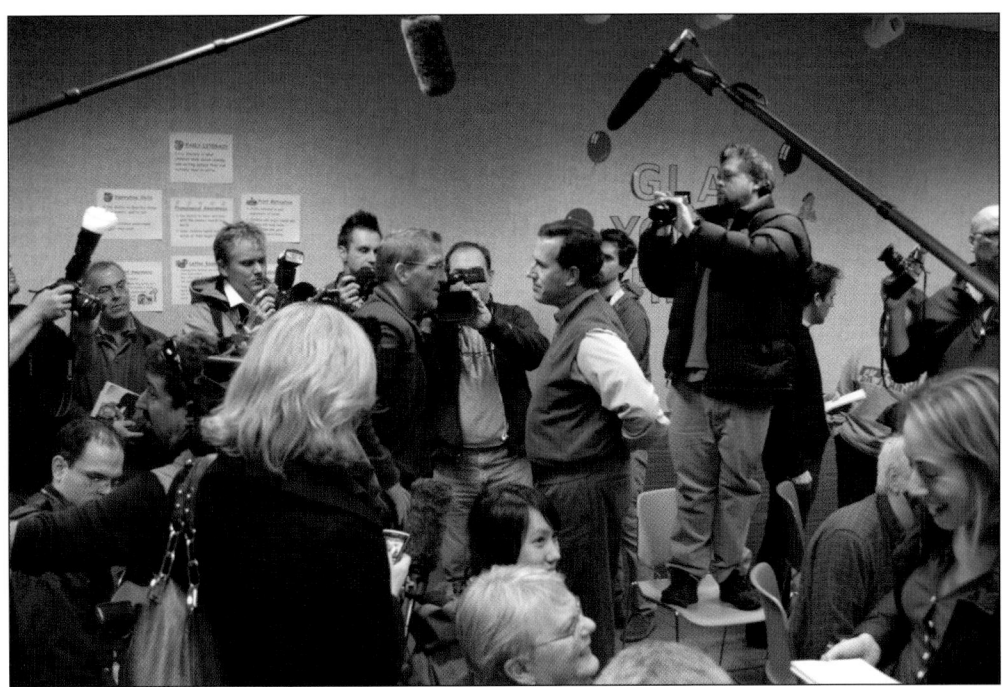

Former senator Rick Santorum gained momentum late in the 2012 Iowa campaign, and media outlets responded with increased coverage. Here, he speaks with an Iowa voter at a public library in Indianola, Iowa. (Author's collection.)

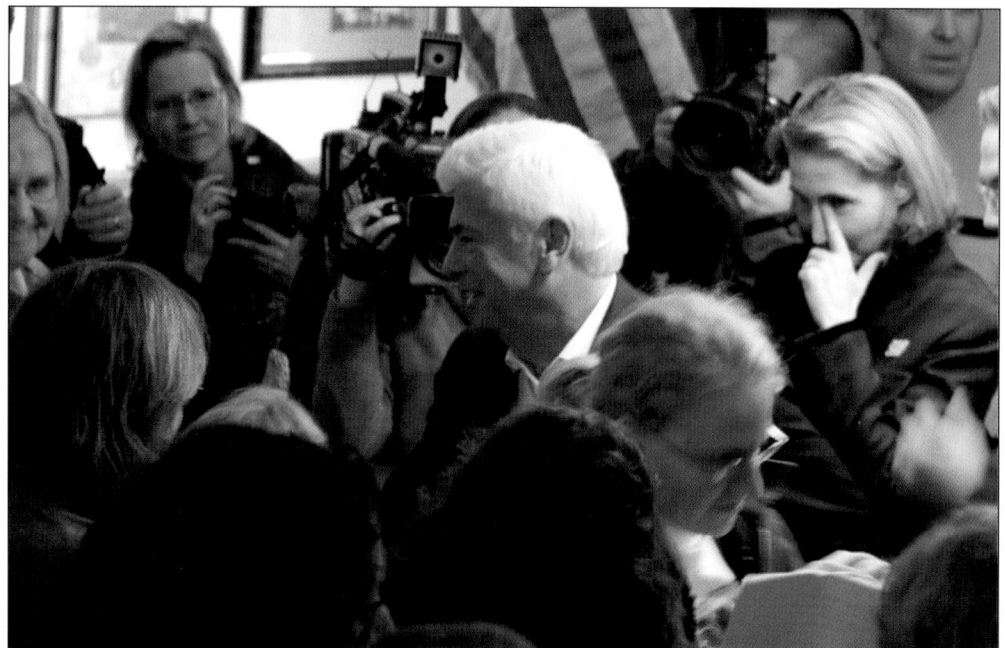

Chris Dodd, pictured here at an event at a restaurant in Indianola, Iowa, purchased a home and moved his family to Iowa in his effort to spend as much time as possible in the state. Although Dodd was not expected to perform well, the media nonetheless came out in full force to cover his campaign in the week prior to the caucuses. (Author's collection.)

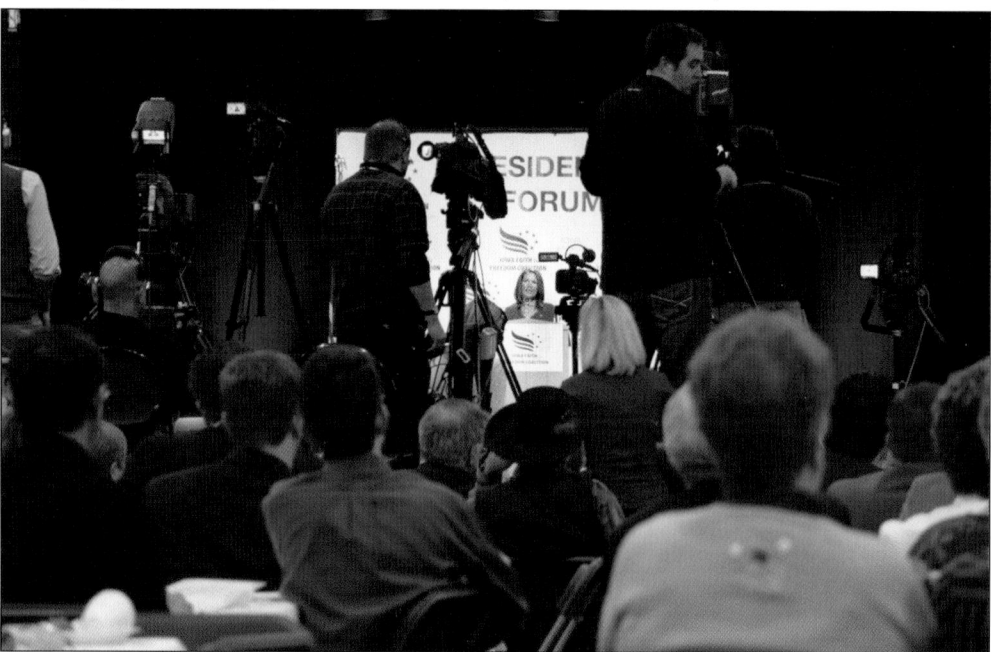

Organizations frequently hold presidential forums, inviting candidates to speak to their members. The Faith and Freedom Coalition, a group advocating social conservativism, attracted all of the major 2012 candidates and a good number of media outlets. Here, Michele Bachmann addresses the crowd. (Author's collection.)

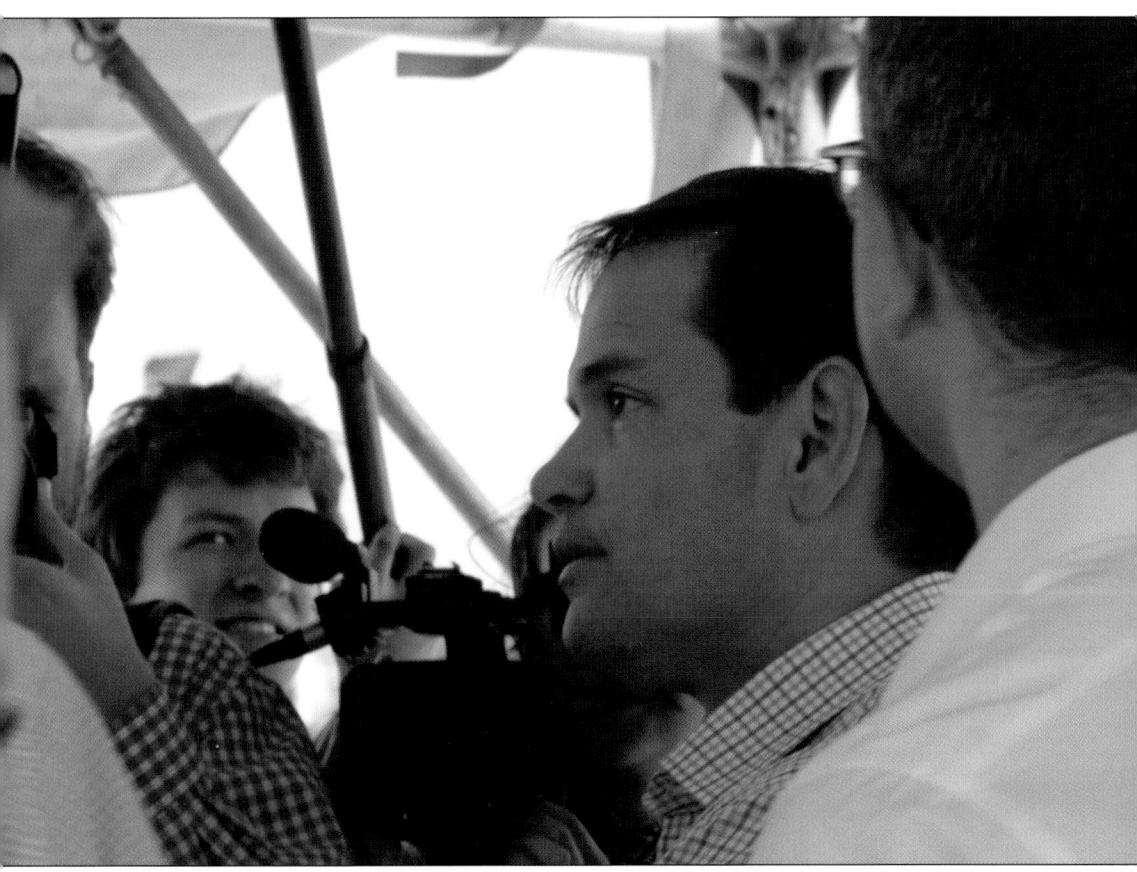

During the first Roast and Ride, a new annual event created by Iowa Republican senator Joni Ernst, the 2016 presidential candidates got their first crack at the national media spotlight. In much the same way that the Harkin Steak Fry galvanized Iowa Democrats, the Roast and Ride, which consisted of a motorcycle ride celebrating veterans and patriots and a pork roast, is expected to continue as a GOP tradition in Iowa. Florida senator Marco Rubio, seen here at the event in Boone, Iowa, is surrounded by supporters and cameras as he heads to the stage. (Author's collection.)

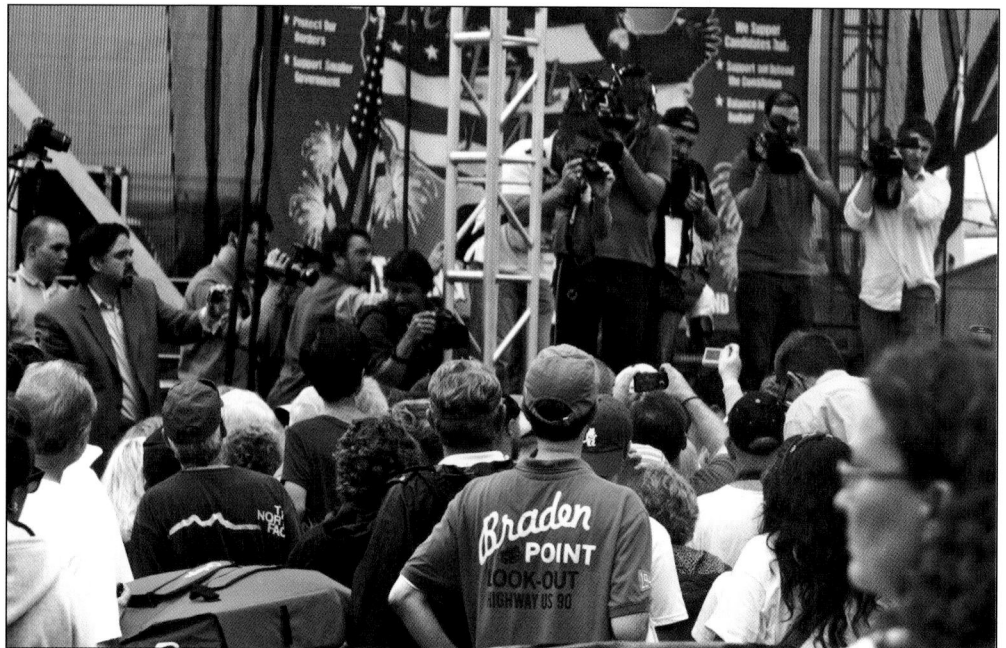

Former vice-presidential candidate Sarah Palin held a rally in Indianola, Iowa, in 2011. Although many expected her to announce her intentions to pursue a 2012 campaign, she did not do so and ultimately decided not to declare her candidacy; nonetheless, the event attracted substantial media attention. (Author's collection.)

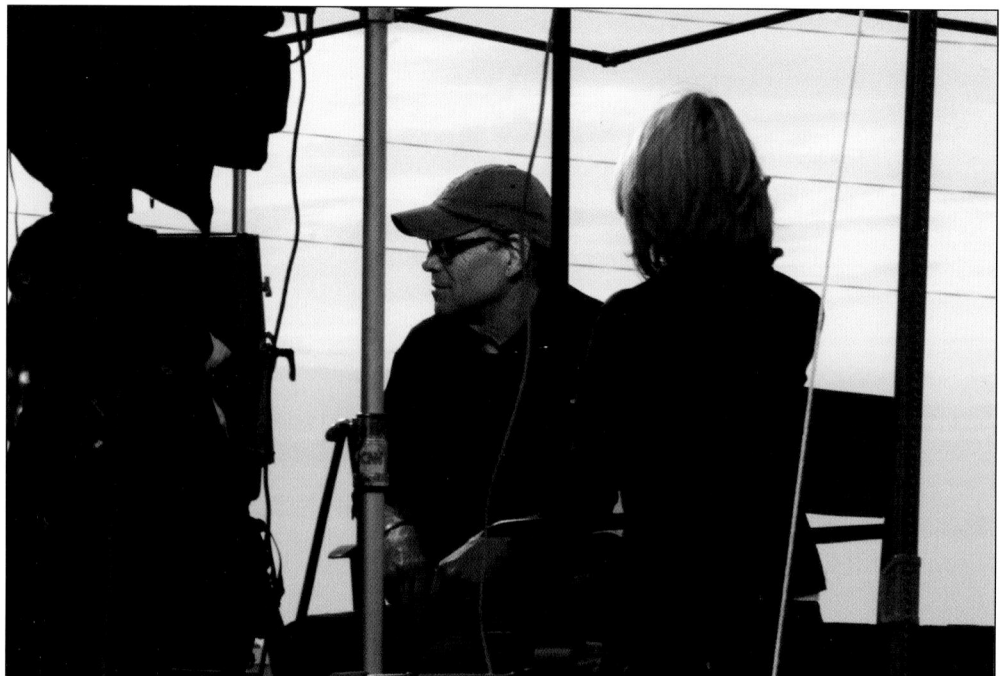

In 2015, newly elected Republican senator Joni Ernst hosted the first Roast and Ride in Boone, Iowa. One media outlet set up an impromptu live set at the event, interviewing candidates while the event was happening. Pictured here is Texas governor Rick Perry. (Author's collection.)

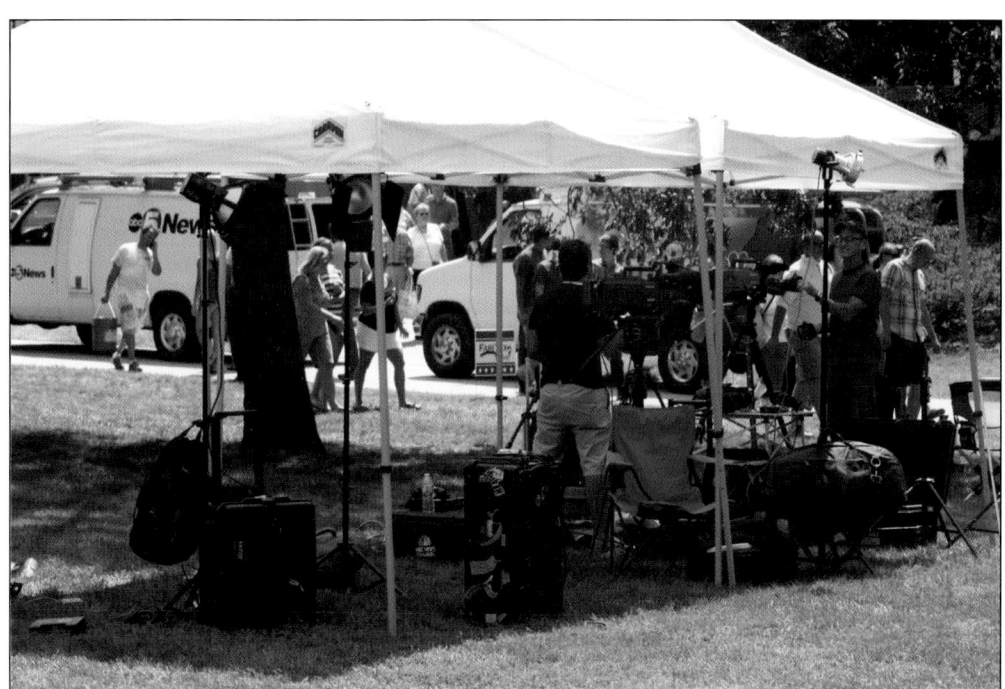

From 1979 until 2011, the Republican Party of Iowa held the Iowa Straw Poll, a fundraiser in Ames that served as an informal test of organizational strength among party activists the summer prior to the caucuses. Media organizations would set up in tents to broadcast live from the straw poll. (Author's collection.)

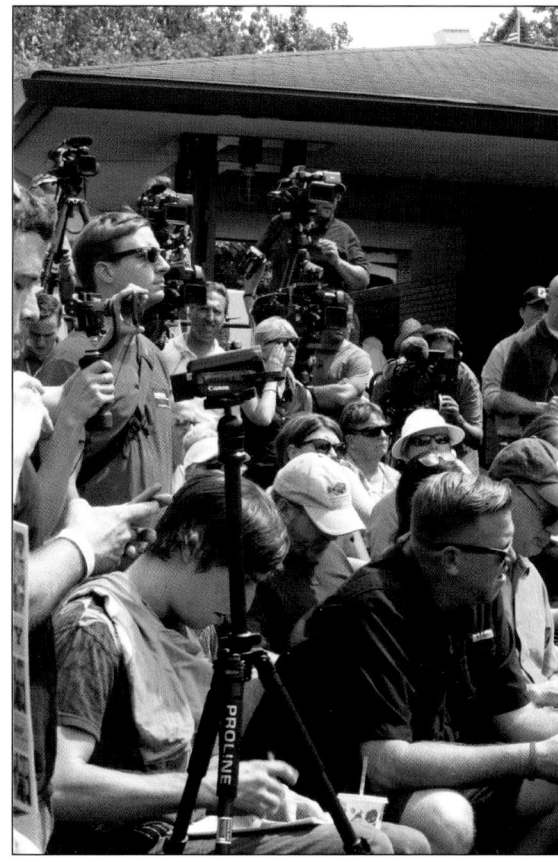

The Iowa State Fair is one of the largest in the country and attracts Iowans from near and far. Every four years, in the summer prior to a presidential caucus, the *Des Moines Register* sets up the soapbox on the grand concourse. In addition to the voters who gather around the stage to hear the candidates, who each have a short time to speak and take questions, media cameras and amateur photographers set up to capture the contenders. (Author's collection.)

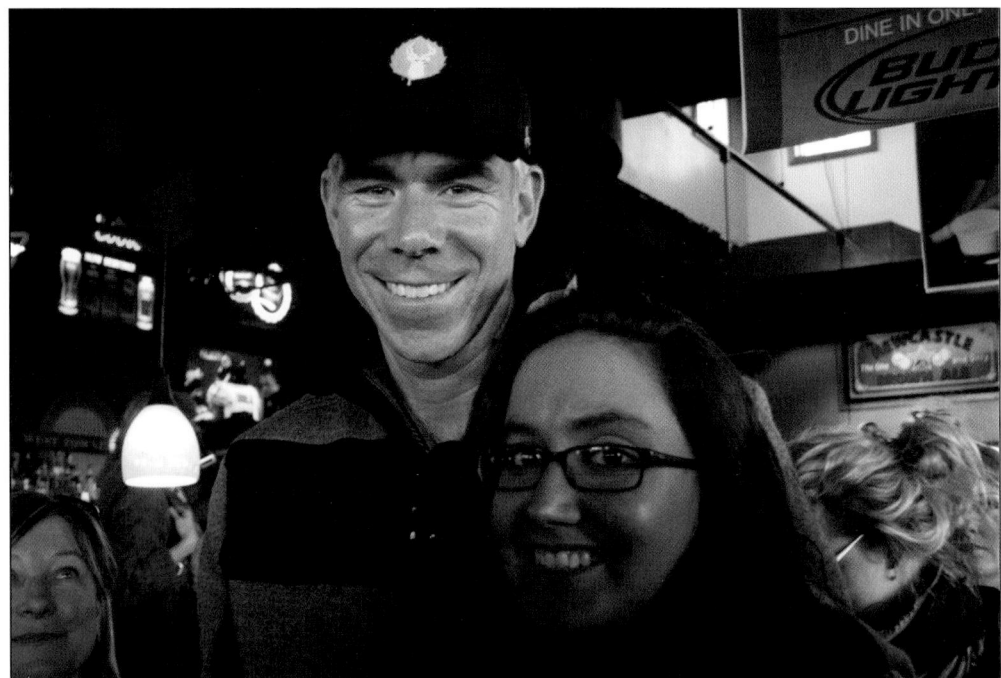

In the weeks prior to the caucuses, national media personalities and party activists want to be on the ground in the state. Pictured here at a 2012 Gingrich campaign event at a local restaurant in Ames, Iowa, is then-national DNC staffer Jill Shesol running into David Gregory, who served as host of NBC's *Meet the Press* at the time. (Author's collection.)

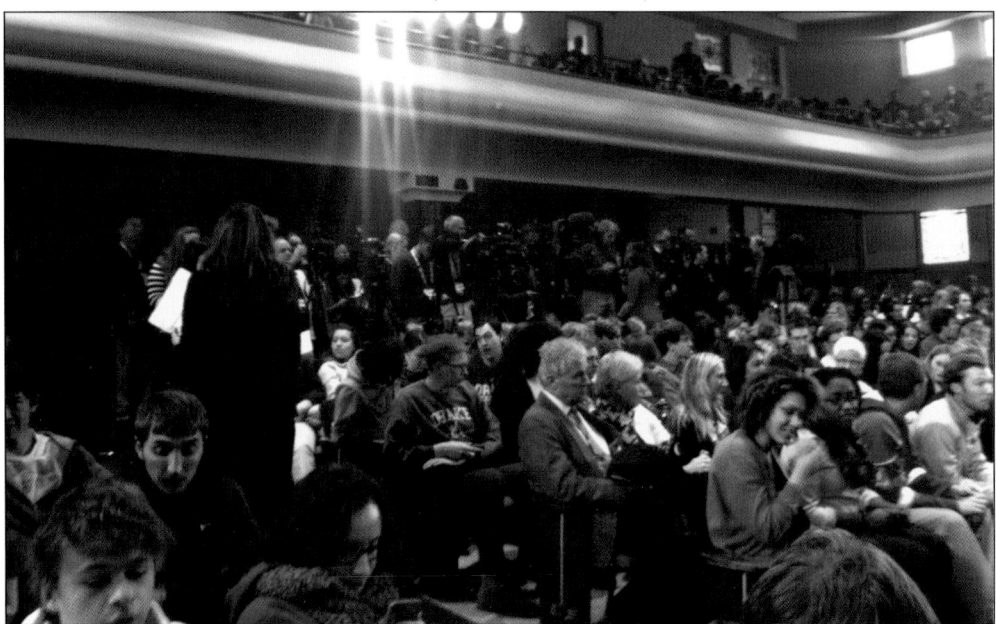

In February 2015, Vice Pres. Joe Biden came to Drake University. After two failed presidential bids in 1988 and 2008, Biden was widely rumored to be considering another run in 2016, and the media packed the back of the auditorium to capture his remarks. Biden announced in October that he would not be a presidential candidate. (Author's collection.)

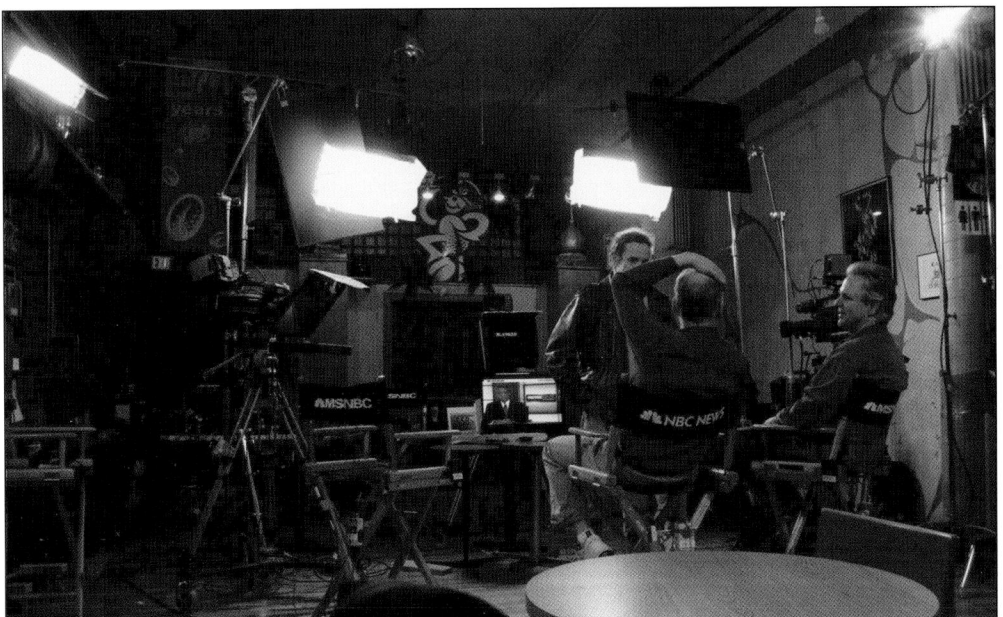

Many national media outlets scout locations for caucus coverage months in advance of caucus night. Here, NBC News established its set in a local Des Moines coffee shop, Java Joe's. Patrons would crowd into the shop to watch live shows broadcast on-site in the days leading up to the 2012 caucuses. (Author's collection.)

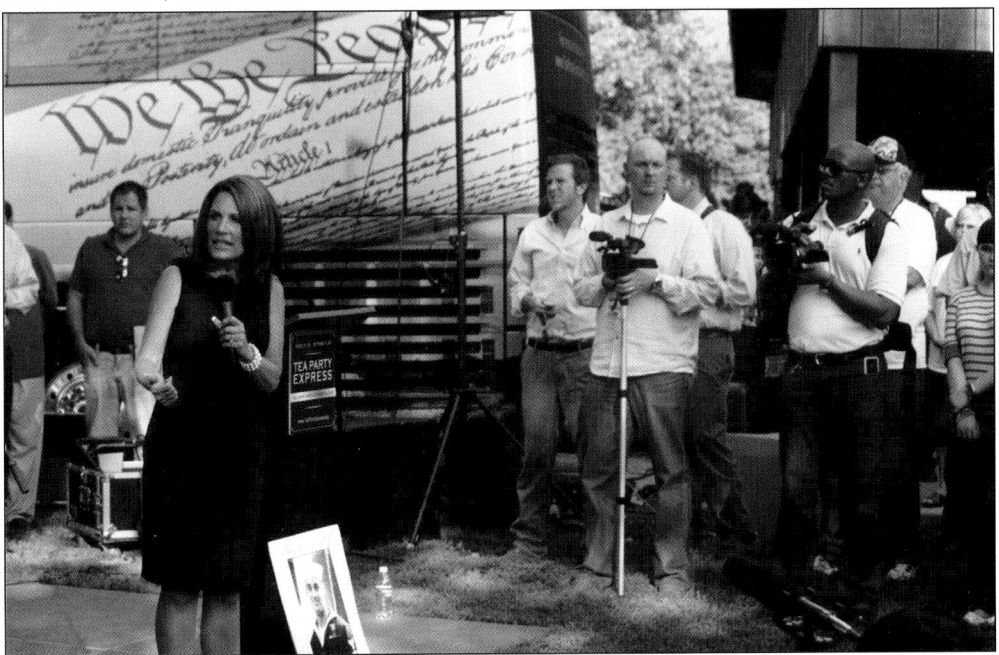

Even before the campaign heats up, cameras appear at small candidate events. Some of the cameras provide footage for national media organizations, while others are used by trackers from competing campaigns or issue groups recording the candidate's comments in the hopes of better contesting the race or documenting the policy positions announced. Michele Bachmann is speaking here at a Tea Party Express event while cameras capture her remarks. (Author's collection.)

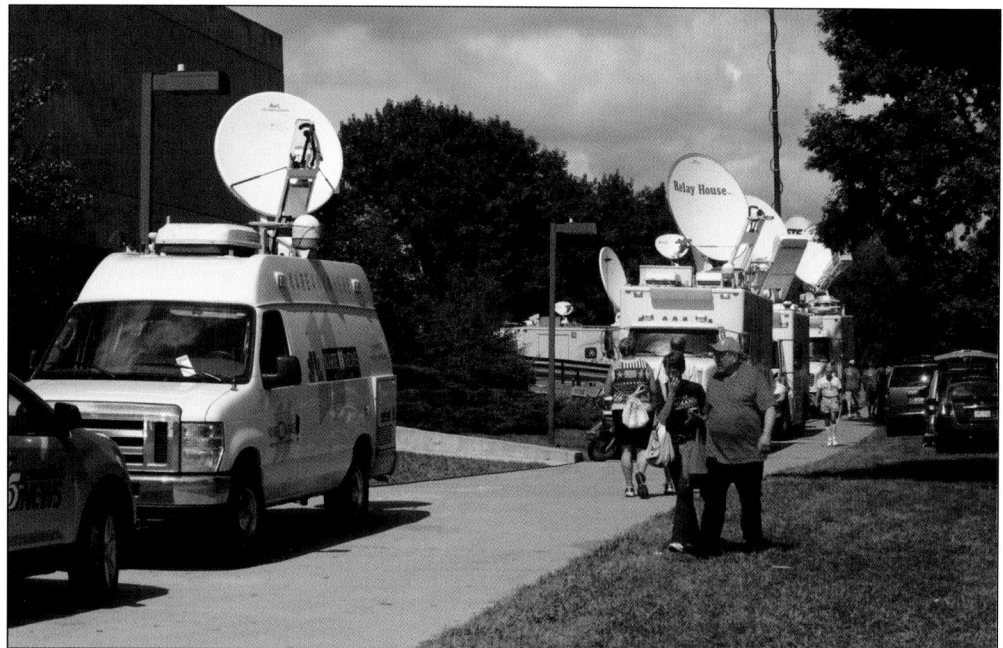

Large events attract national media attention, and satellite trucks become a regular feature of life in Iowa. Here, satellite trucks line the walkway at the 2011 Iowa Straw Poll. The 1987 straw poll included just 3,843 votes; in 2011, with a very competitive field, 16,892 voters cast ballots in the informal preference poll. (Author's collection.)

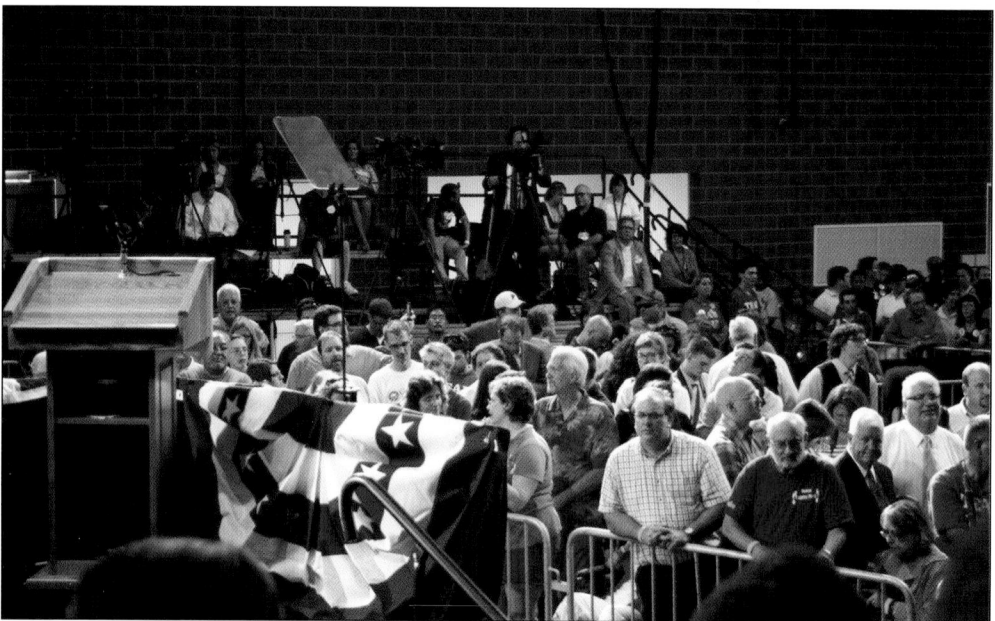

The early days of the caucus campaign features small events, but in the later stages large rallies are more common, particularly for incumbents running for reelection. President Obama did not face a caucus challenger in 2012, but he held large campaign events prior to the general election. Like most events, it included a press riser, and many video cameras set up early to ensure a good shot of President Obama. (Author's collection.)

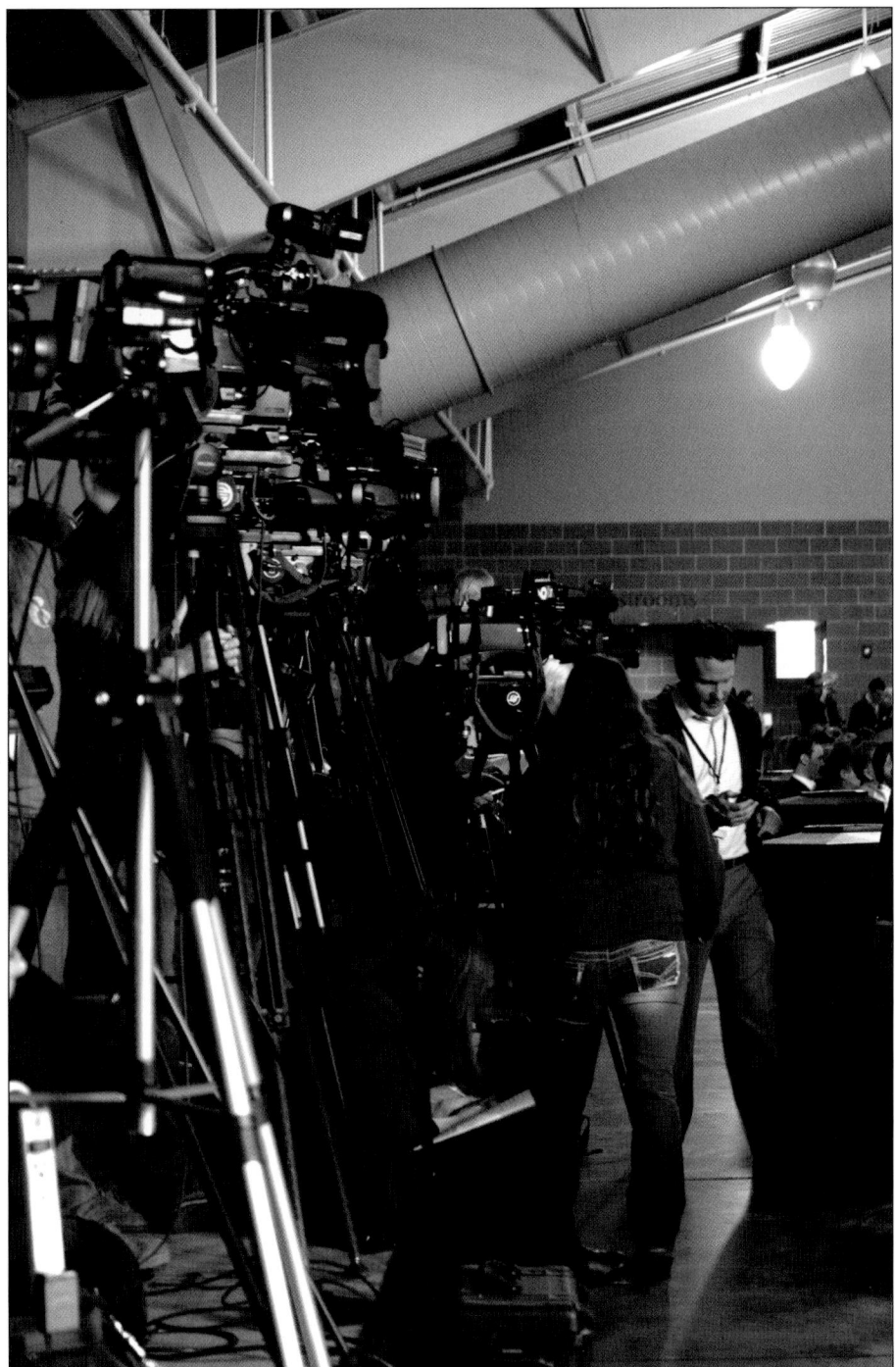

Every major event provides a location for print journalists to report to their local, state, national, and international media outlets. In addition, the media riser, where cameras can set up, offers a clear view to the stage. Cameras often compete for limited space and create a striking line, as they did at the 2015 Iowa Ag Summit, which allowed an early glimpse of nine Republican candidates. (Author's collection.)

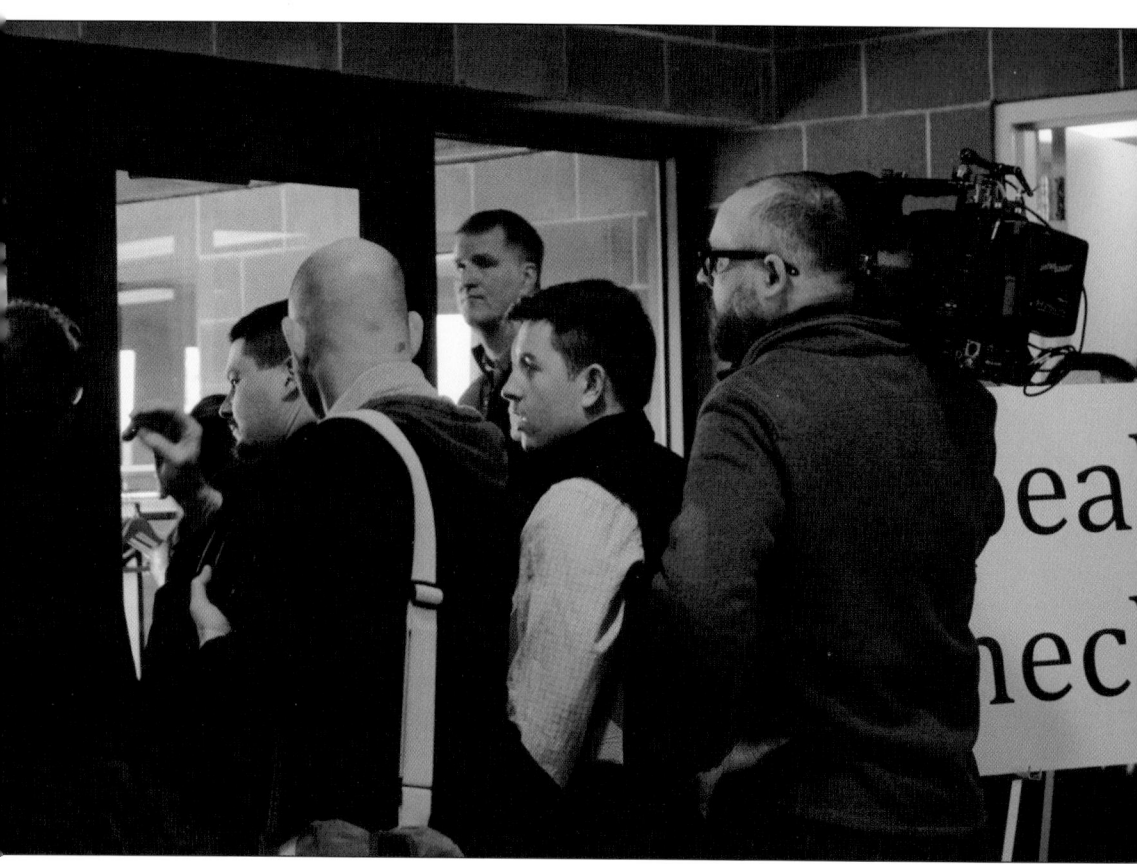

Camera operators quickly learn the entry and exit points to any event and crowd around the door to gain proximity to the candidate in the hopes of getting good footage or a chance to ask questions. This scrum awaits the entrance of Jeb Bush at a 2015 event at the Iowa State Fairgrounds. (Author's collection.)

Five

ALL EYES ON IOWA

If one is thinking of becoming president some day, it is important to get to know Iowa. Contrary to conventional wisdom, the state is not flat; gentle rolling hills comprise most of the landscape. The characteristics that define the state are, in many ways, just like those that exist in any American state: its people are hardworking, pragmatic, and community-minded. Some have described Iowa citizens as quintessentially nice. Attitudes and values are generally consistent with the Midwestern United States: stability, consistency, and modesty are important. Like other Midwestern states, Iowa has witnessed the decimation of the manufacturing base, and small towns struggle to compete for good jobs and economic opportunities. In many of Iowa's cities and towns, there is a healthy dose of Normal Rockwell's America; town squares serve as the center of civic activities, aging dime stores and stately steeples serve as landmarks, and family-owned restaurants, diners, and ice-cream parlors serve as gathering places. It is an unpretentious place.

Although Iowa has some things in common with other states, it differs in the unique role it plays in the nation's political life. Iowans take this role seriously. For some, that means putting issues on the agenda. For others, it means working for a campaign. And many more simply turn out to meet candidates, listen to what they have to say, and make their best judgment about who can best lead the country. Along the way, there are some quirky moments on the Iowa campaign trail. Iowans see candid backstage moments with presidential contenders. Costumed protesters show up on the streets outside campaign events. Costumed supporters show up at campaign events dressed as the founding fathers. Campaign staff set up bales of hay in urban office parks to appease national media reporters looking for that "Iowa" shot. Handwritten signs show up at all events. Red, white, and blue clothing is more common at political events than one might expect.

The opportunities for political engagement in Iowa bring many campaign staff to the state and have contributed to a growing base of young professionals in Iowa's cities. Unemployment in Iowa is just 3.8 percent, and the capital city of Des Moines has been listed on a number of top-10 lists, including *Forbes* best city for young professionals in 2014.

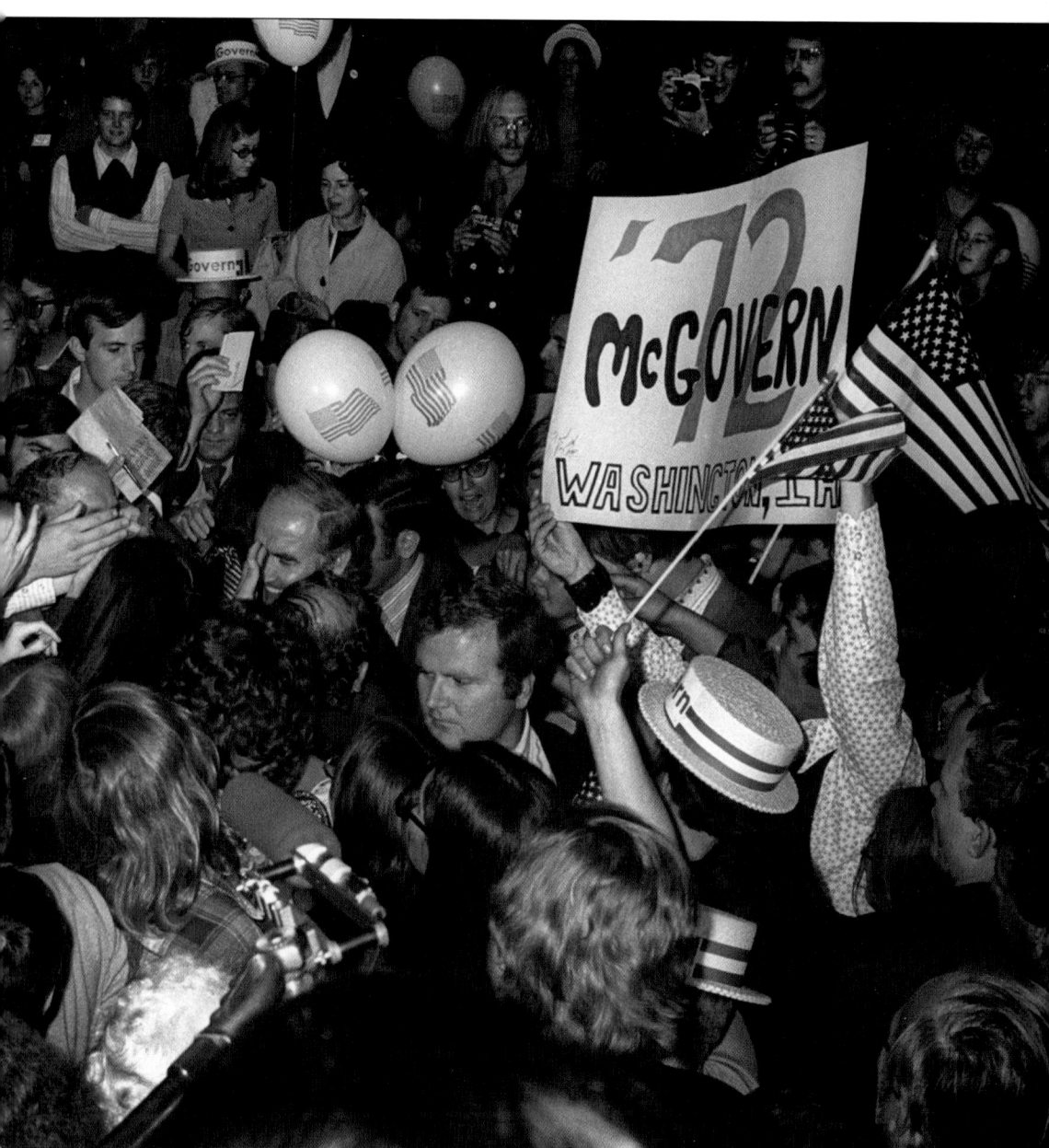

Following the 1968 convention, Democratic party reforms were led by George McGovern, who went on to win the Democratic nomination in 1972. Although Jimmy Carter was the first to draw significant attention to the caucus process, McGovern's campaign (with campaign manager Gary Hart at the helm) focused on states that held caucuses, believing they would be less expensive for the campaign. McGovern used Iowa as a launching pad for his presidential bid. He had a strong third-place finish in the caucuses. At the time, before the national spotlight focused on the Iowa caucuses as a winnowing process and the national media came to think of Iowa as a do-or-die contest, this was strong enough. (Courtesy of Keith Wessel.)

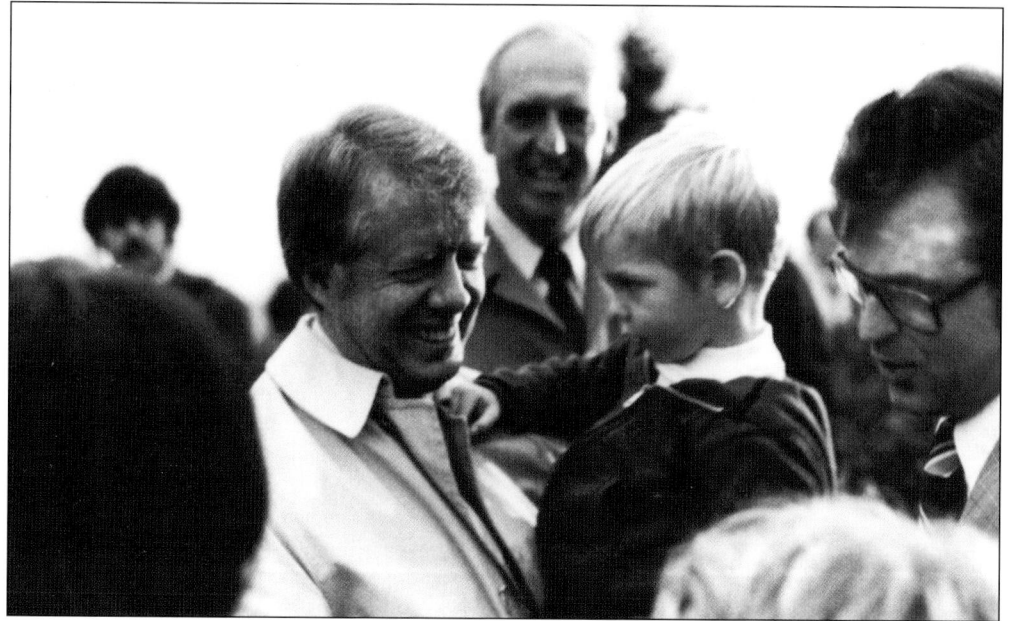

The Iowa caucuses first gained attention when Jimmy Carter outperformed expectations in 1976. Here, he meets a young supporter at a campaign event during his 1979 reelection campaign. Although Carter did not win the caucuses in 1976, the extensive time that he spent in the state led to an overwhelming win against Ted Kennedy in 1980. (Courtesy of the Harkin Collection, Drake University Archives and Special Collections.)

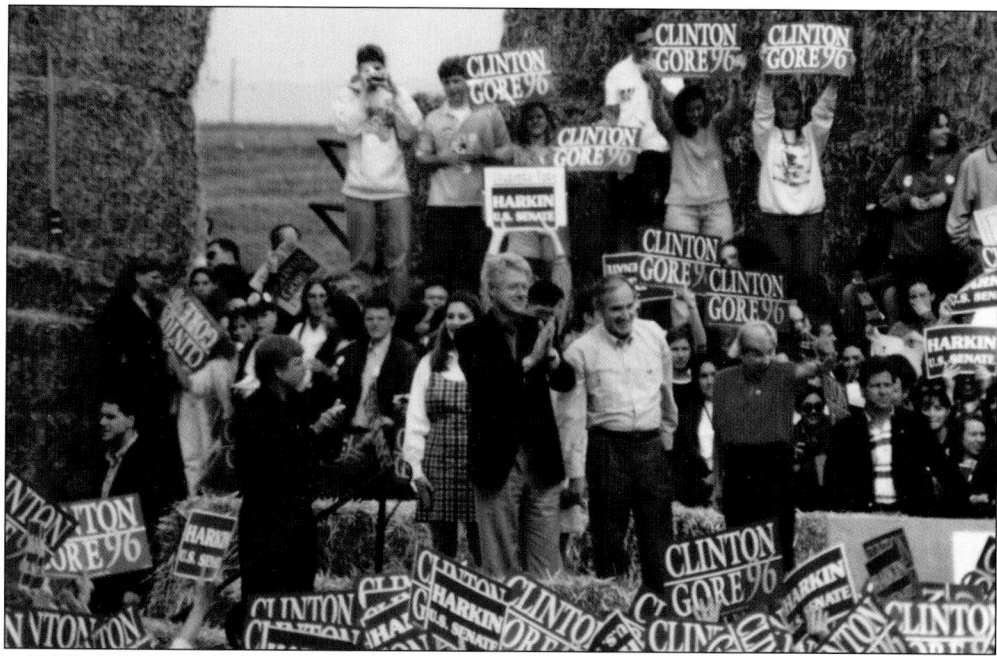

Bill Clinton spent little time in Iowa during his 1992 campaign because home-state senator Tom Harkin was sure to win. During Clinton's 1996 reelection campaign, the two former rivals joined forces at a campaign event in Iowa. (Courtesy of the Harkin Collection, Drake University Archives and Special Collections.)

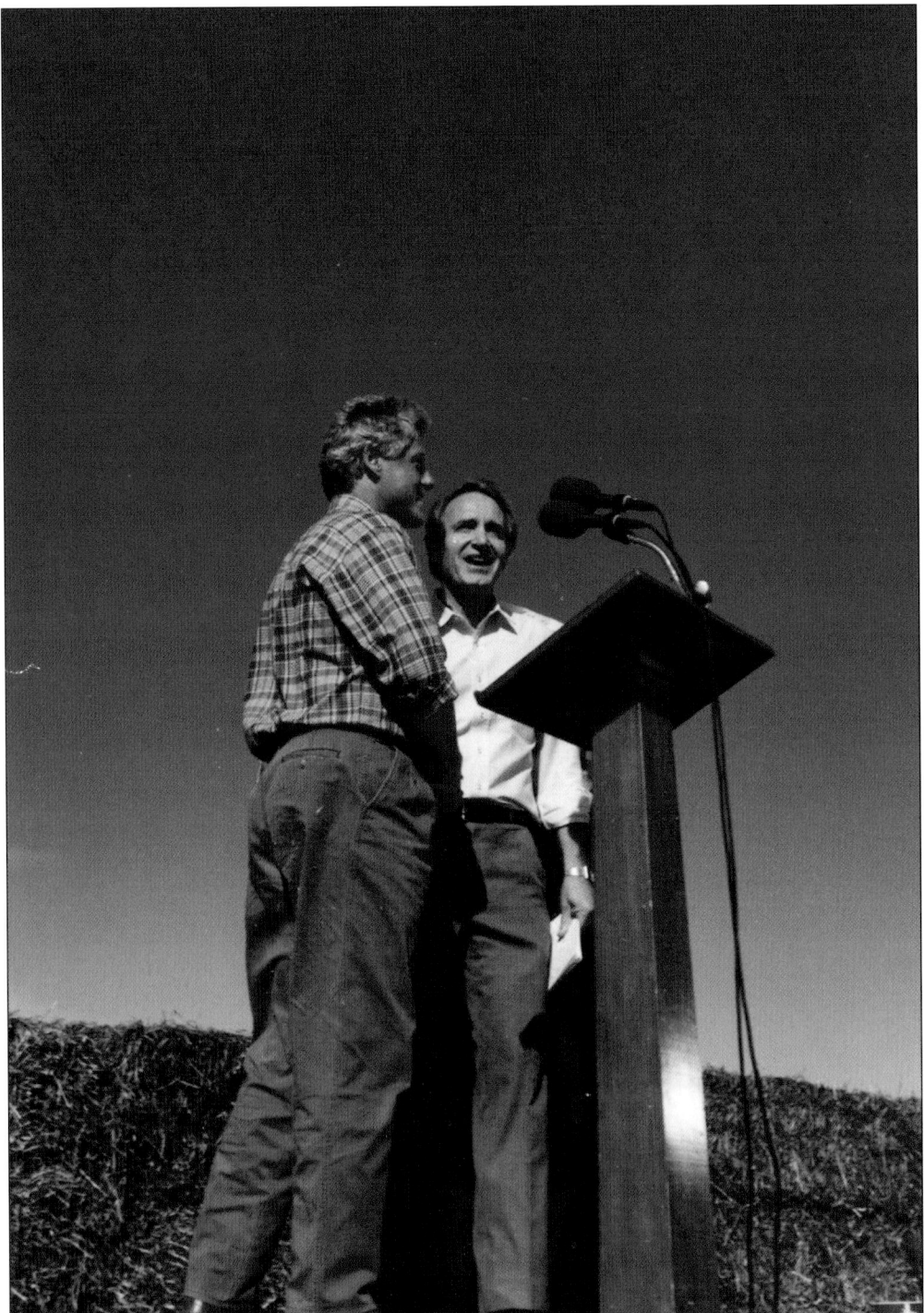

After a failed bid for the presidency, Sen. Tom Harkin welcomed former opponent and winner of the Democratic nomination Bill Clinton to the Harkin Steak Fry in 1992 during the general election campaign. Clinton would go on to win the presidency and return to the steak fry two more times. (Courtesy of the Harkin Collection, Drake University Archives and Special Collections.)

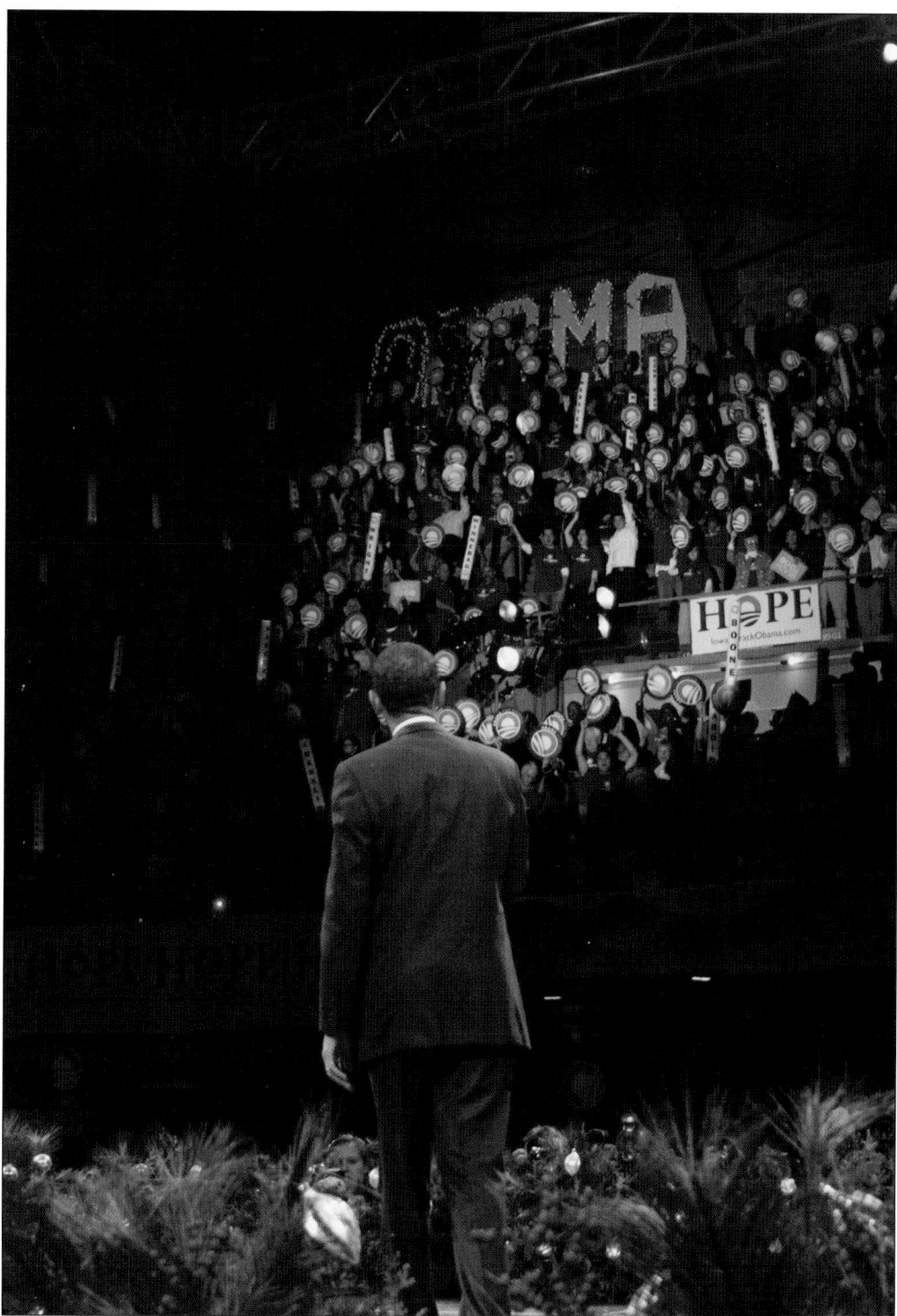

Barack Obama's win in Iowa in 2008 propelled his campaign forward nationwide. In 2012, he returned to the state during his reelection campaign and attracted huge crowds at rallies across the state. (Courtesy of Jordan Oster.)

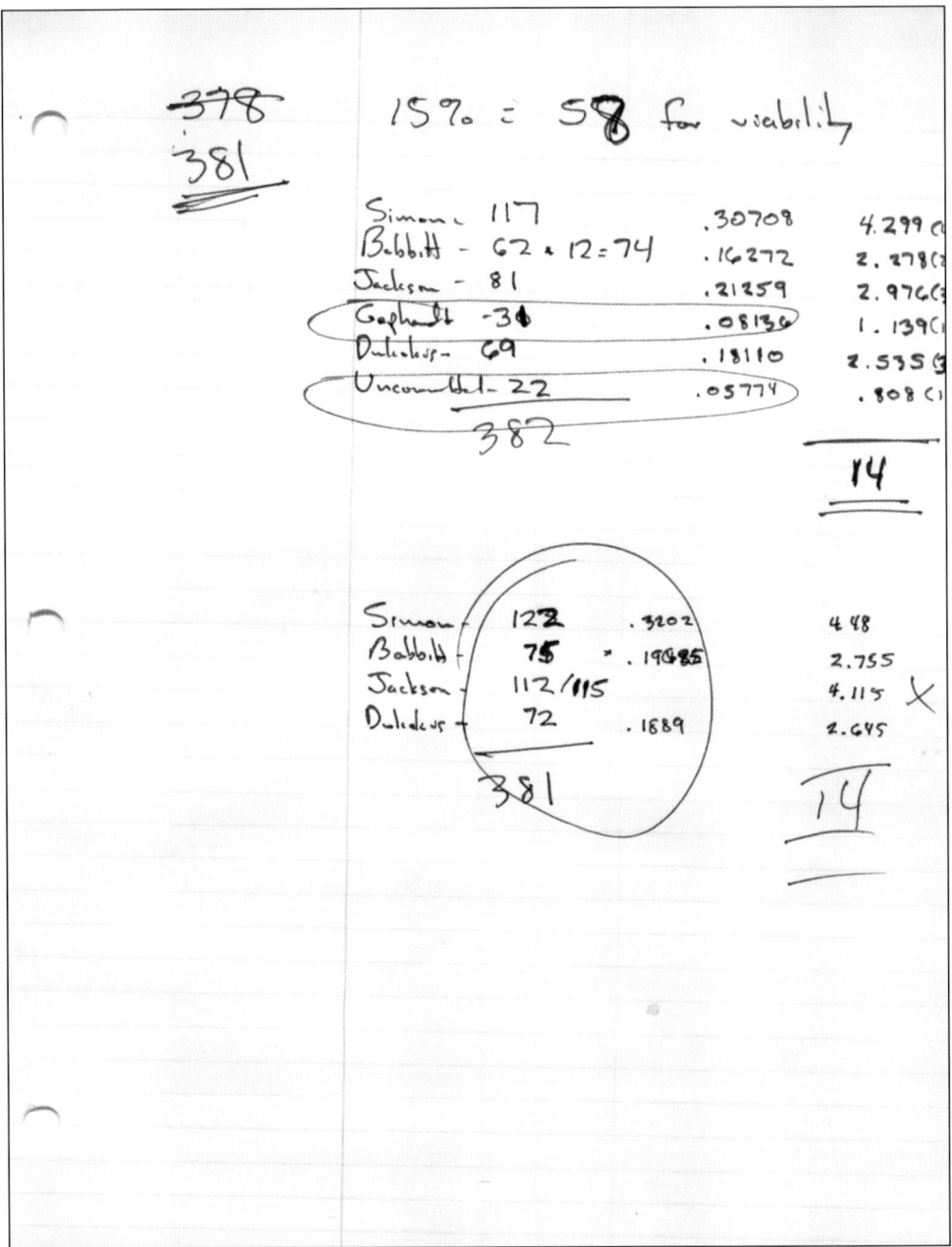

Despite the national attention Iowa's caucuses receive, they are local meetings run by local volunteers. Unlike primaries, caucus results are tabulated by volunteer caucus chairs. In the Democratic caucuses, the results are determined through a system of caucus math, and delegates to the county conventions are awarded based on proportional representation, with a viability threshold of 15 percent. Here, a caucus chair has determined the results of the 1988 caucuses. (Courtesy of the Iowa Caucus Collection, Drake University Archives and Special Collections.)

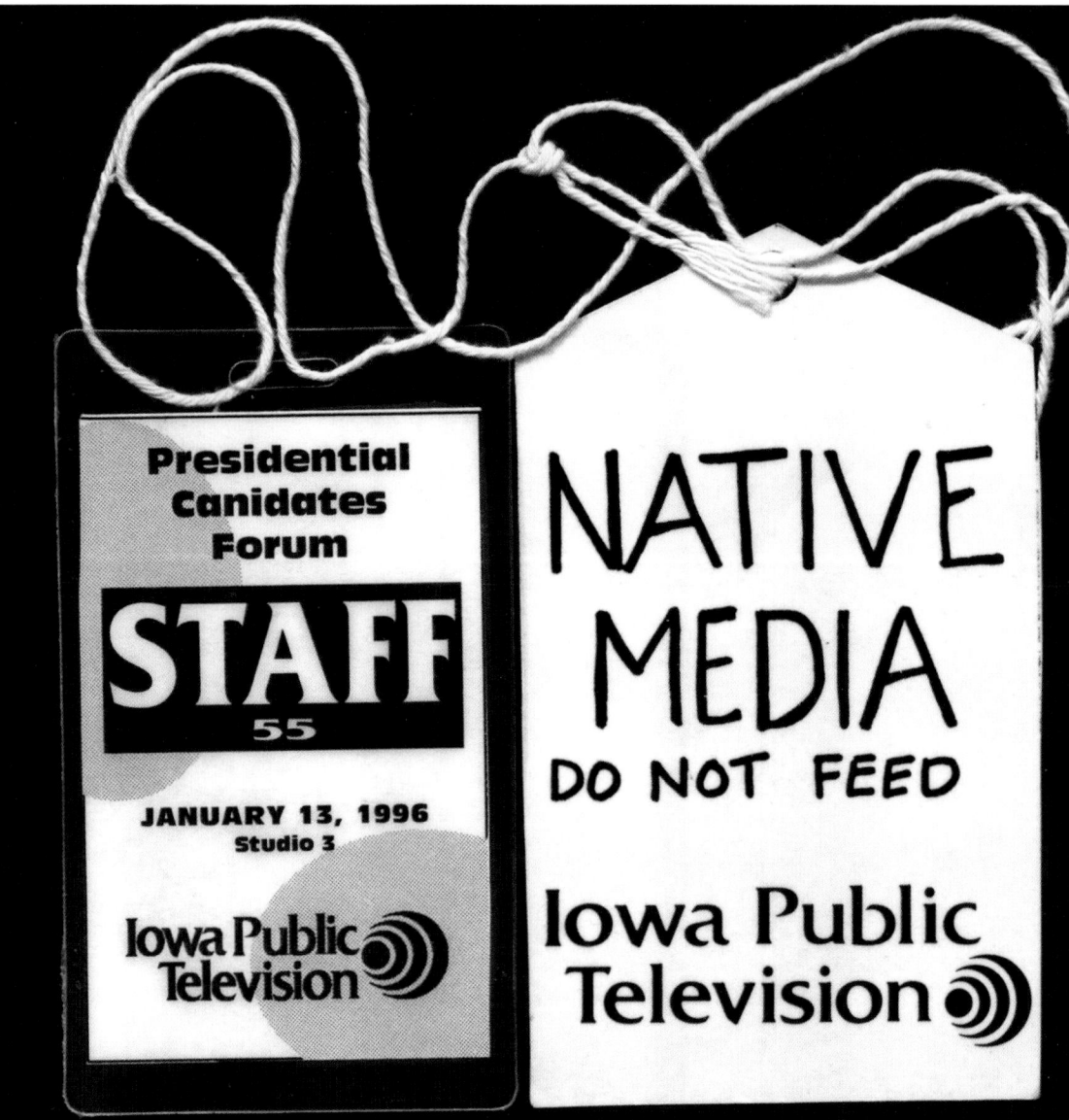

When asked to characterize Iowa, many people simply refer to the people as nice, and self-deprecating humor is a part of this reputation. At the 1996 Iowa Public Television forum, local media added a homemade credential-poking pun at themselves, reminding visitors not to feed them. (Courtesy of the Iowa Caucus Collection, Drake University Archives and Special Collections.)

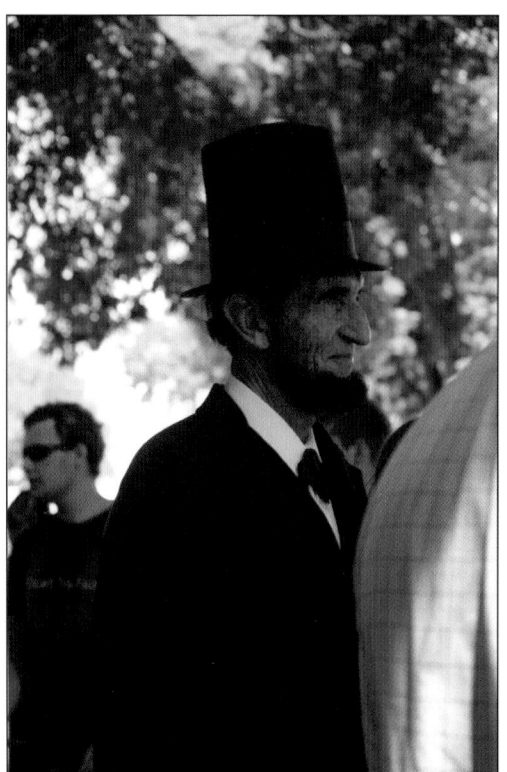

It is not uncommon to encounter the occasional historical figure at campaign and party events in Iowa. In August 2011, an actor portraying Abe Lincoln had a line of people asking for photographs at the Republican Party's Iowa Straw Poll. (Author's collection.)

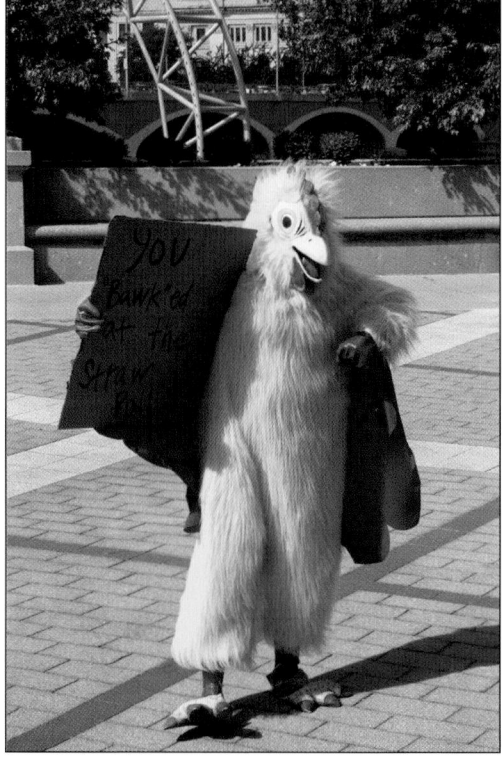

Not attending the 2007 Iowa Straw Poll was a strategic decision by former New York mayor Rudy Giuliani. But competing campaigns called attention to his decision by inferring that he was chicken, appearing outside a Giuliani Fiscal Responsibility policy address in downtown Des Moines. (Courtesy of Jordan Oster.)

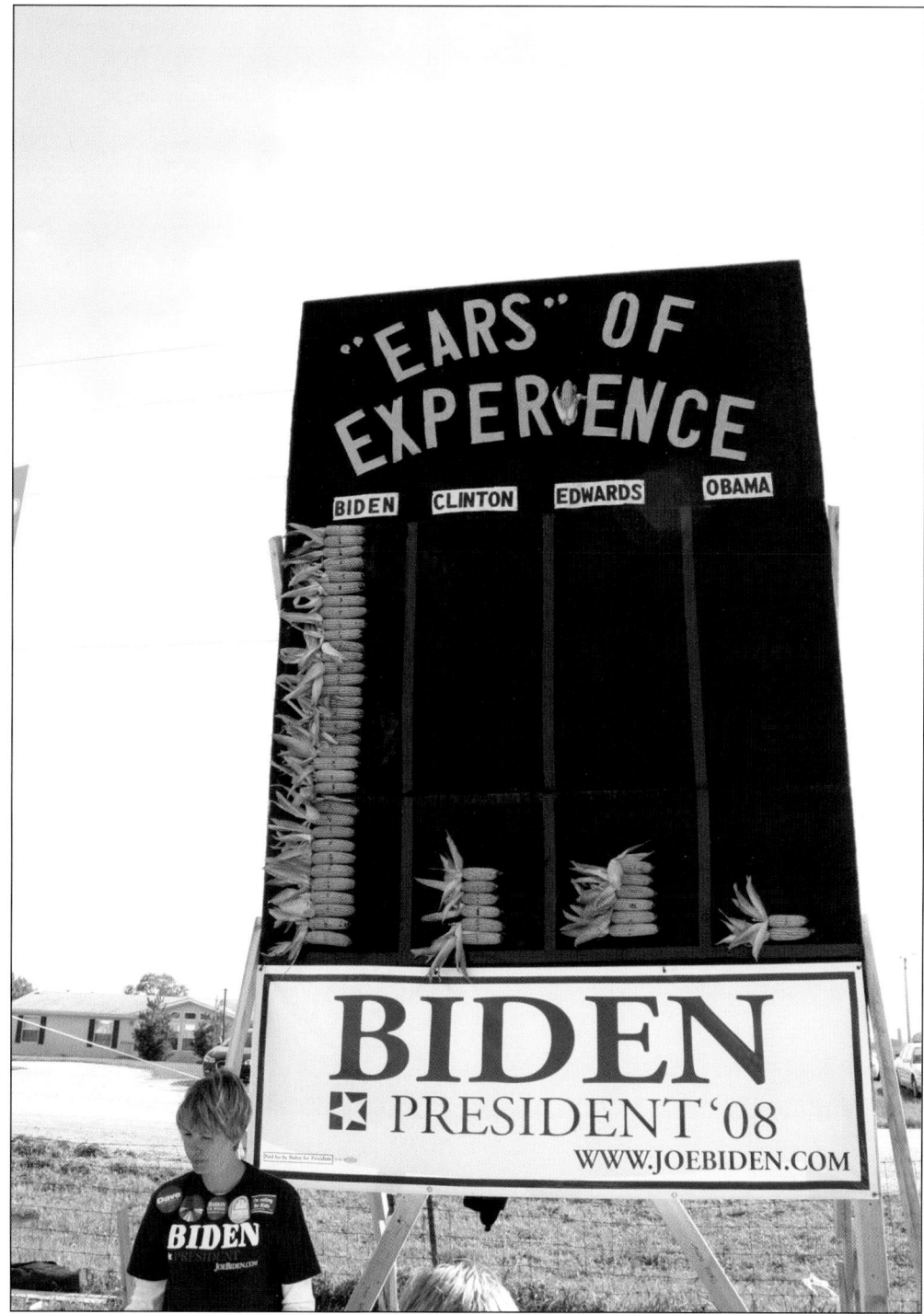

Any number of informal contests appear throughout the state in the year preceding a presidential election, from the kernel poll run by a local television station at the Iowa State Fair to the coffee bean poll at Iowa City's Hamburg Inn No. 2. Here, the Biden campaign creates a corn-themed display to argue that their candidate is more experienced. (Courtesy of Jordan Oster.)

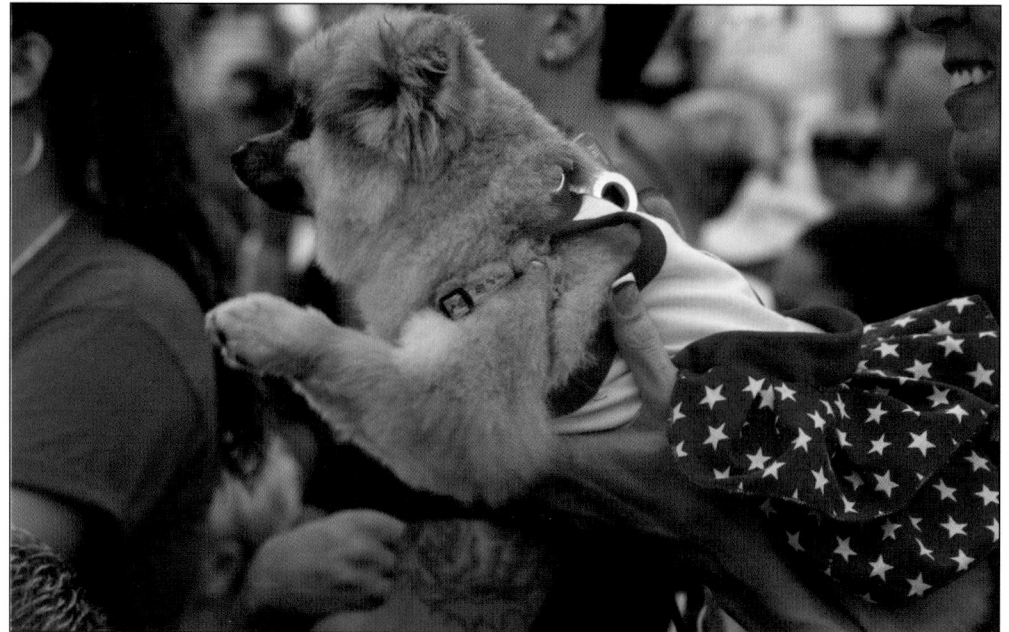

Costumes to demonstrate patriotism at campaign events are not limited to human voters. Seen at a Tea Party rally in Indianola, this pup has been thoroughly outfitted for the campaign season. (Author's collection.)

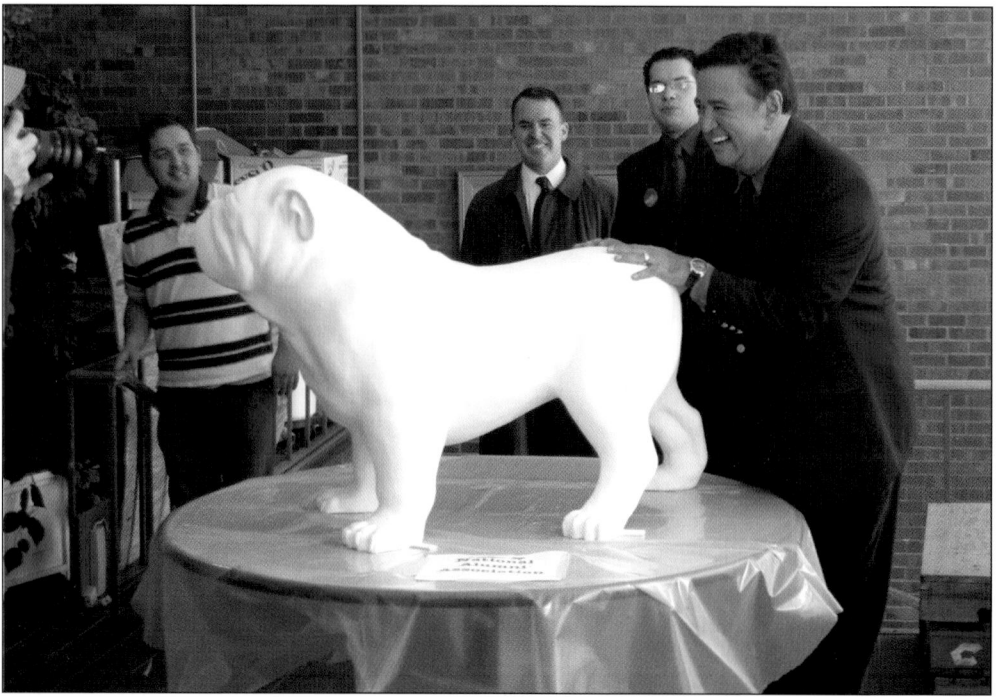

Few voters get to see as many candid moments as Iowans experience. Here, Bill Richardson jokes with Drake University students about their bulldog mascot prior to his appearance on campus in 2007. Richardson took questions from students for two hours during the first week of the semester. (Courtesy of Jordan Oster.)

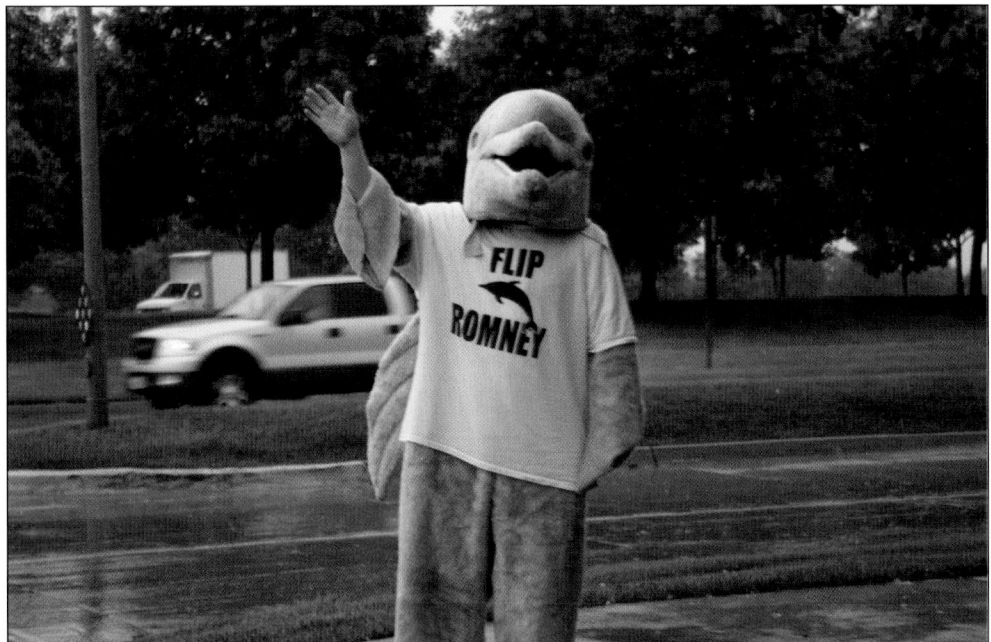

Two activists from a rival campaign appeared outside an "Ask Mitt Anything" town hall meeting held in West Des Moines in 2007. Romney, who was frequently charged with flip-flopping, went on to lose the Iowa caucuses to Mike Huckabee, though he would later become the party nominee in 2012. (Courtesy of Jordan Oster.)

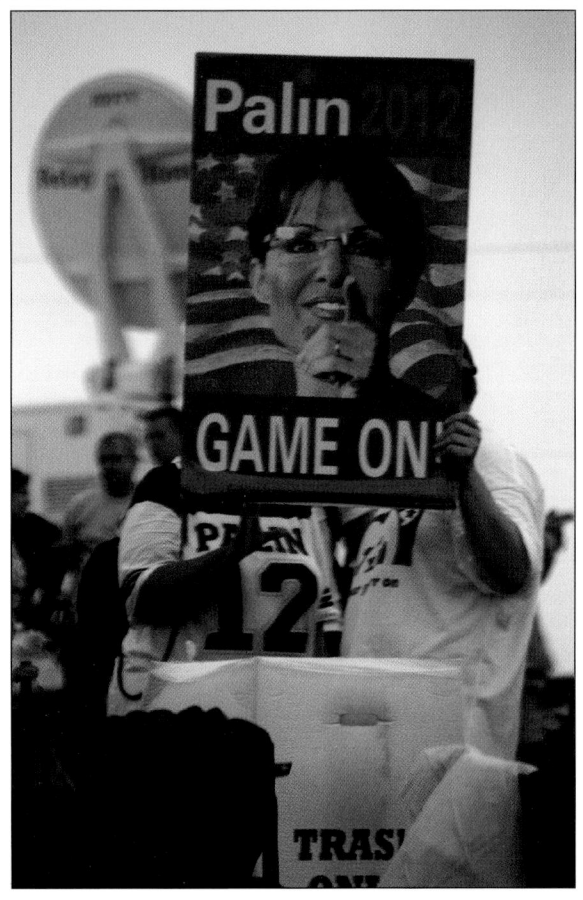

Long before candidates formally announce their intent to run, Iowans regularly turn out to see potential presidential contenders. In 2011, former vice-presidential candidate Sarah Palin visited Iowa on several occasions, including a rally at the balloon field in Indianola. The crowd of approximately 500 to 600 supporters turned out in the rain to support her potential 2012 presidential campaign. Ultimately, Palin decided not to run. (Author's collection.)

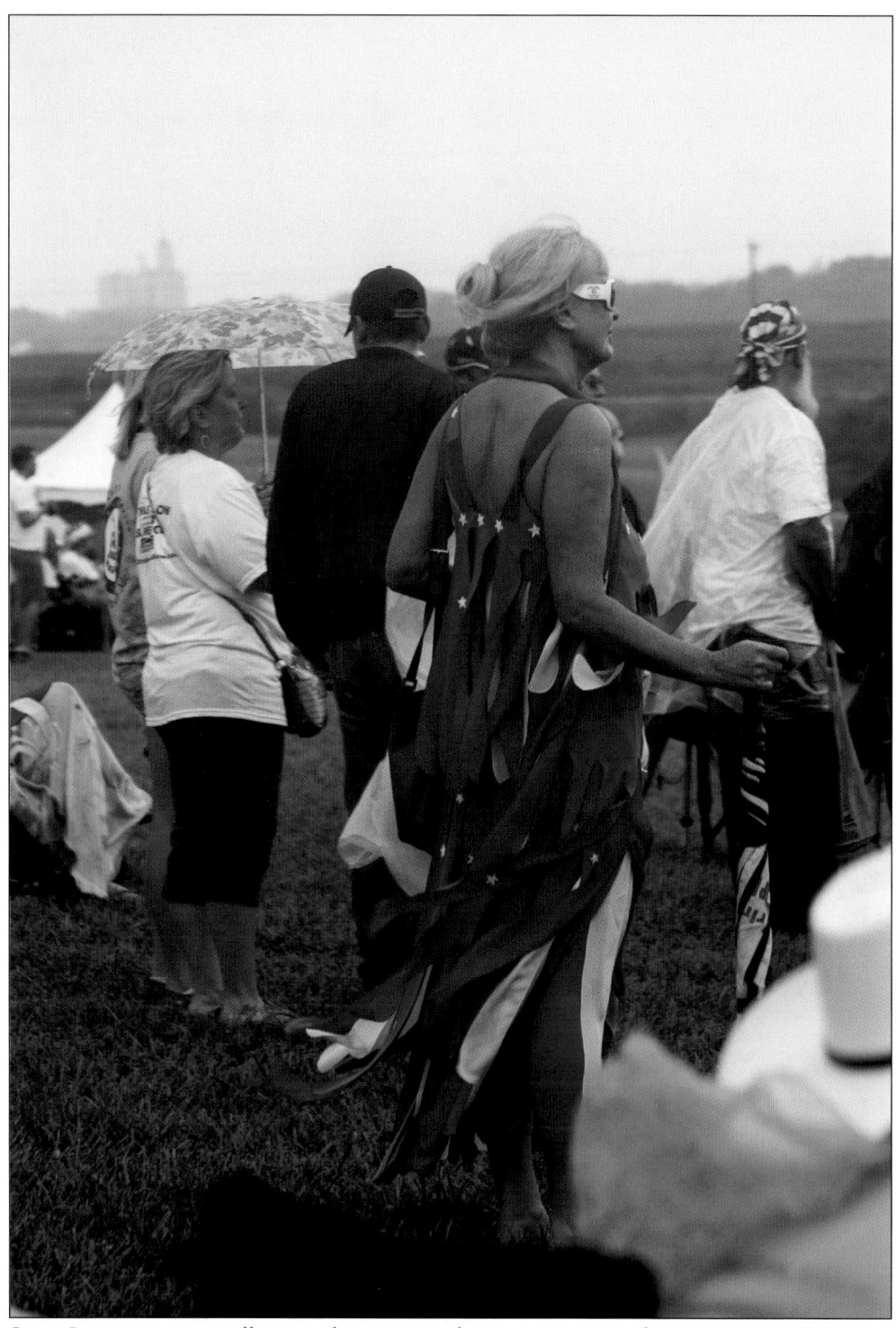

Some Iowa activists go all out to demonstrate their patriotism on the campaign trail. Here, a woman attending a Tea Party event in south-central Iowa dons a special dress for the occasion. (Author's collection.)

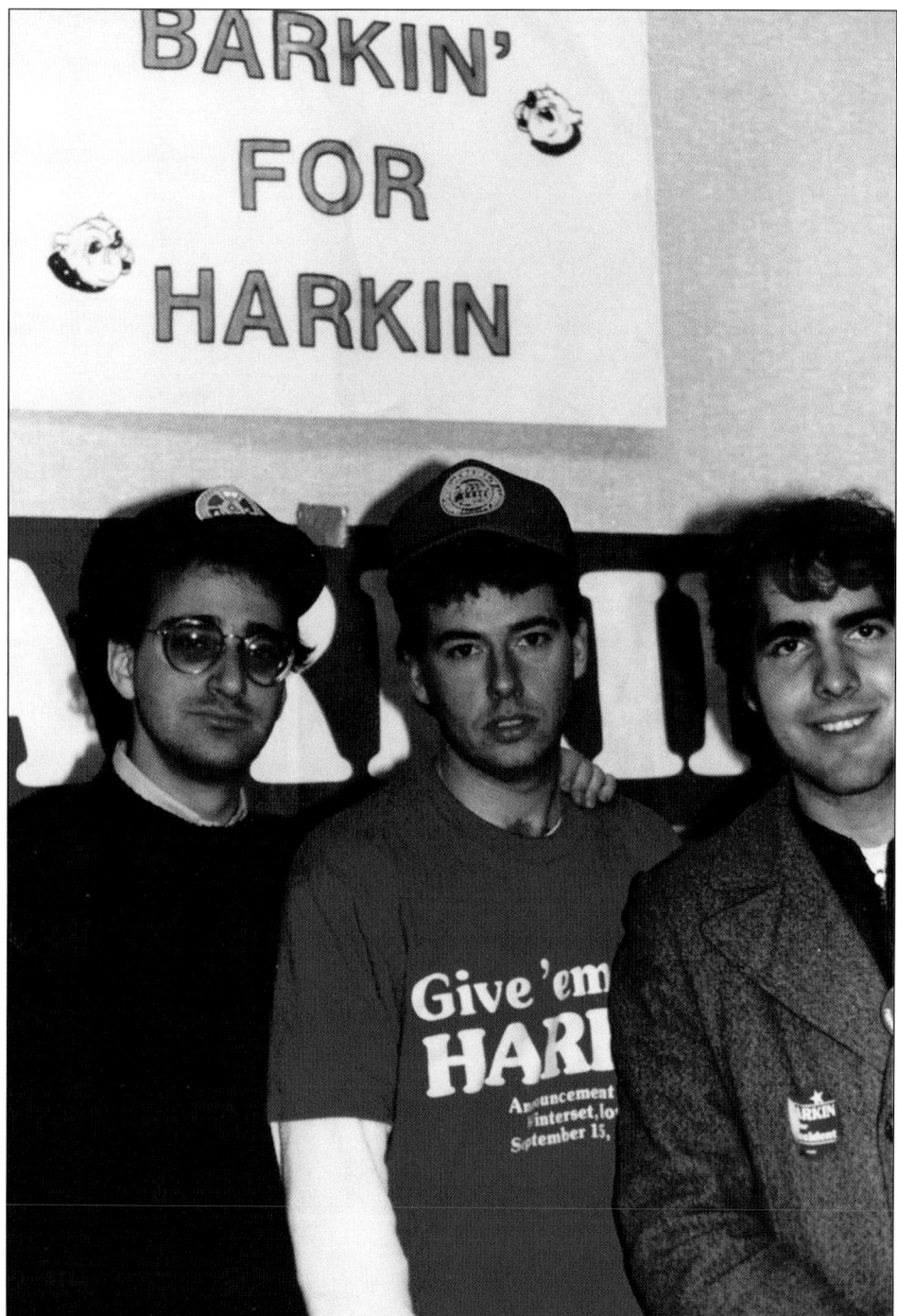

These three young activists were working on the Harkin for President campaign in 1991. Pictured in the center (in the well-known "Give 'em hell Harkin" T-shirt) is David Plouffe, who would go on to become a staffer for Senator Harkin. He is widely known as the campaign manager for Barack Obama's historic 2008 campaign and became senior advisor to the president in 2011. (Courtesy of the Harkin Collection, Drake University Archives and Special Collections.)

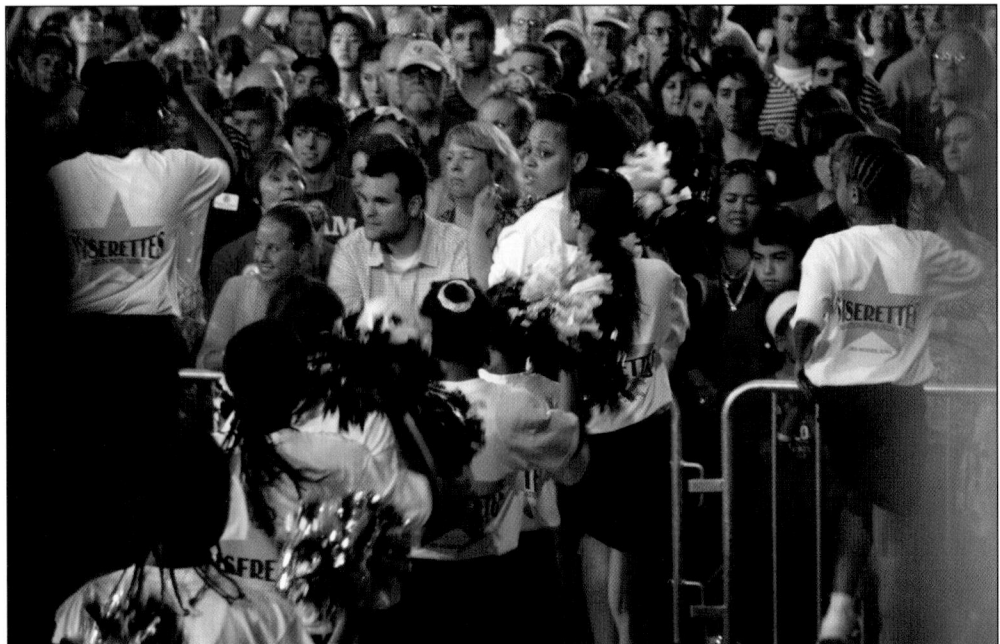

The Isiserettes, a youth drill and drum corps made up of minority students in the Des Moines area with the goal of building character and social skills, are frequent guests at political events around Iowa. Here, they appear at Barack Obama's caucus-night rally after his win. They went on to perform in the inaugural parade and visit the White House. (Author's collection.)

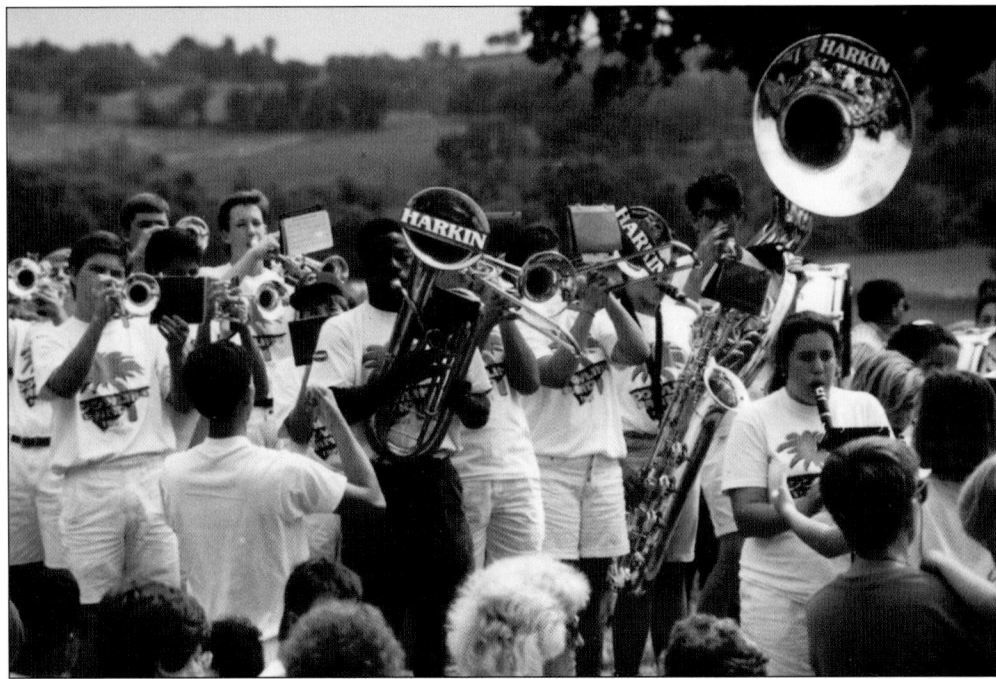

A local high school band appears at the Harkin Steak Fry in Winterset at Tom Harkin's announcement that he would seek the Democratic nomination for president in 1991. (Courtesy of the Harkin Collection, Drake University Archives and Special Collections.)

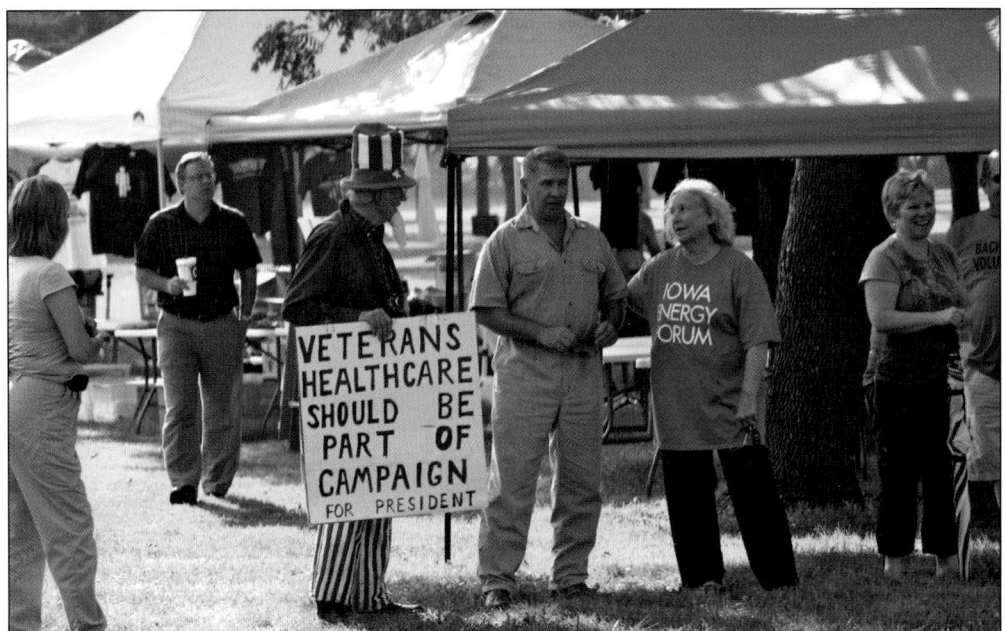

Attendees await a rally with Michele Bachmann in WaterWorks Park in 2007. One man, a military veteran who appears at campaign events for both Democrats and Republicans dressed as Uncle Sam, seeks to put veteran's health care on the agenda for the campaign. Another woman volunteers with the Iowa Energy Forum, a trade organization seeking to shape candidate positions on energy policy. (Author's collection.)

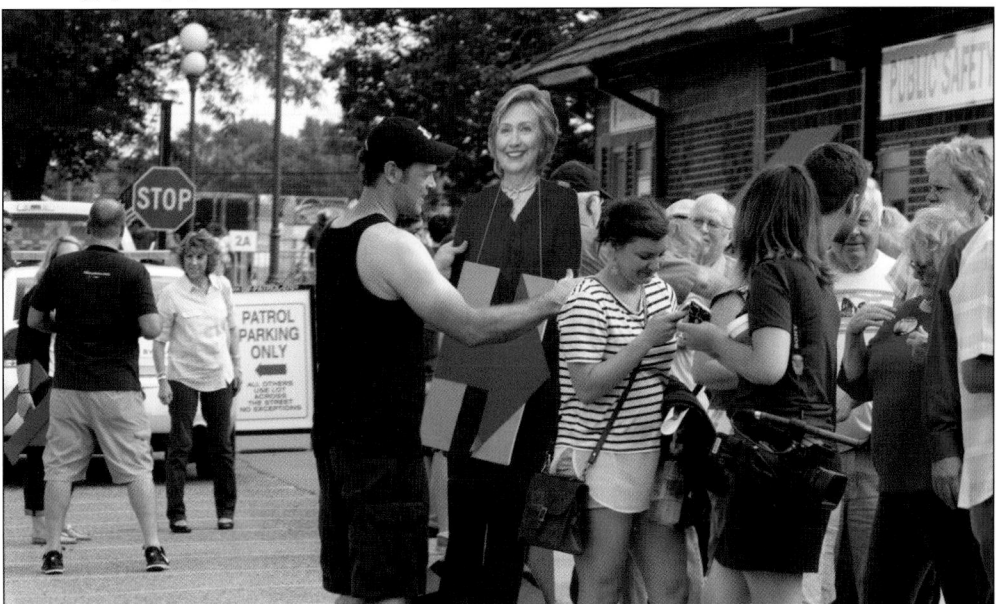

In the fall of 2014, Hillary Clinton returned to Iowa for the first time since her 2008 third-place finish on caucus night. In the spring of 2015, she launched her second campaign for the presidency. Outside campaign events over the summer, her supporters gathered in line to take photographs with a cardboard cutout of the former First Lady, senator, and secretary of state. (Author's collection.)

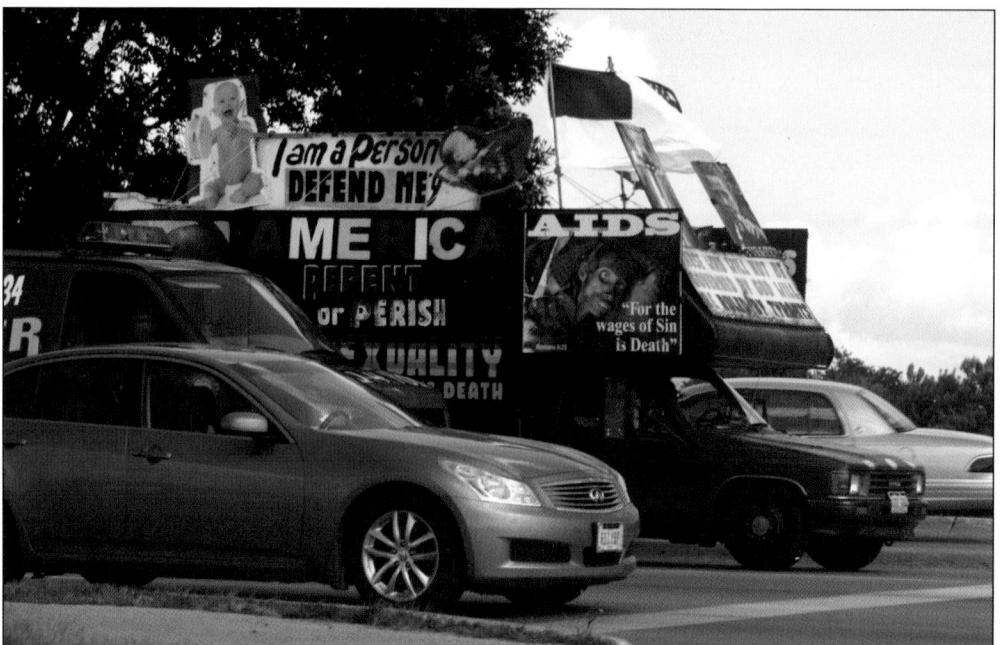

Issue campaigns set up at events around the state, and the state is well known for its active Christian conservative voters who participate in the caucuses. Some 57 percent of Republican caucus attendees in 2012 self-identified as evangelical or born again. Here, anti-abortion protesters drive a very visible campaign truck outside the Ames Straw Poll. (Author's collection.)

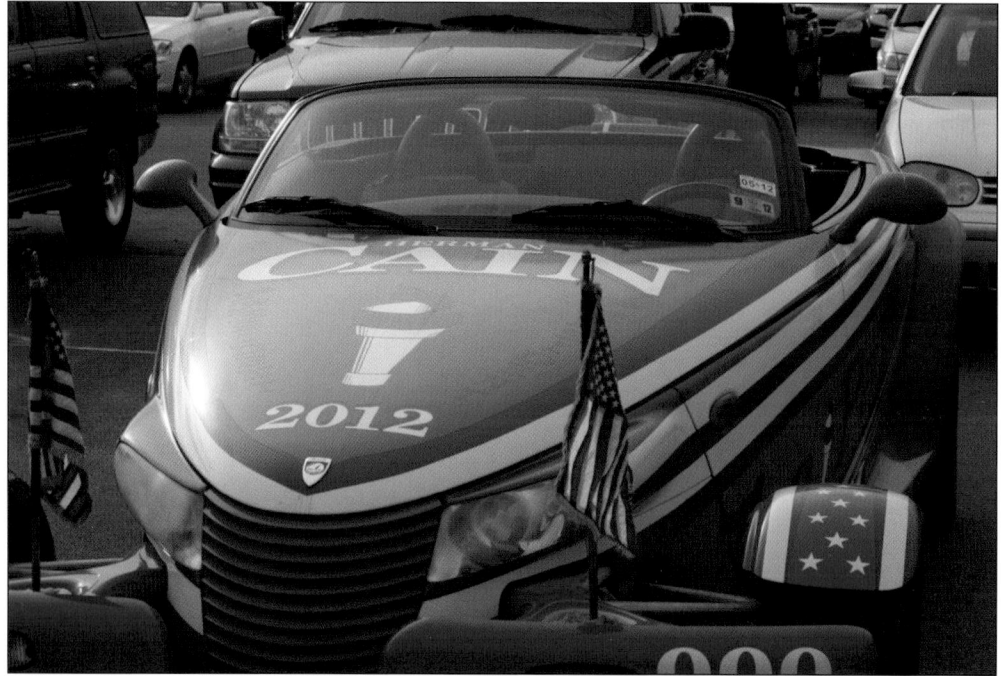

One never knows what he or she will find at an Iowa campaign event, from founding fathers to custom cars. This Cain car was parked outside the Iowa Faith and Freedom Coalition dinner at the state fairgrounds in 2011. (Author's collection.)

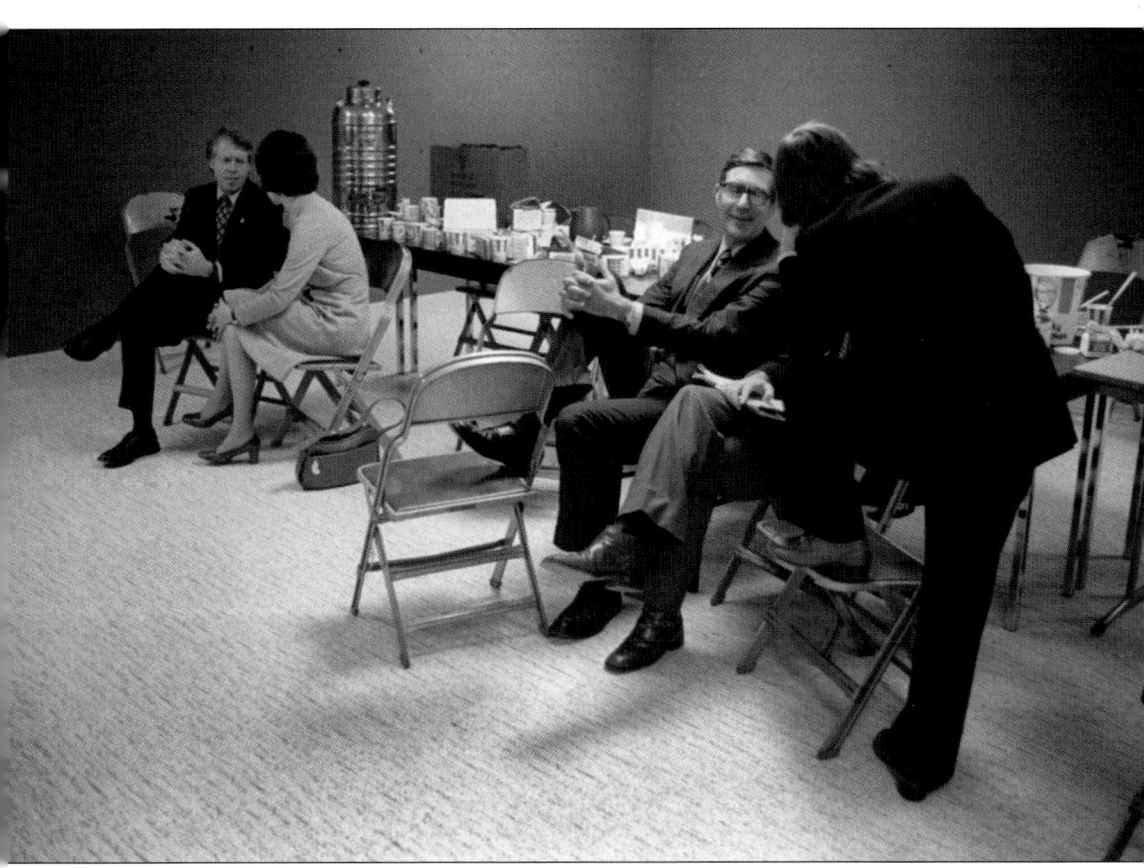

The Iowa campaign is a test of humility for many candidates, even those who have achieved remarkable professional accomplishments. Quiet behind-the-scenes moments on the campaign trail are not glamorous or exciting, as illustrated by this simple tableau with Jimmy Carter and Mo Udall waiting for their time in the spotlight in 1976. (Courtesy of Keith Wessel.)

Discover Thousands of Local History Books
Featuring Millions of Vintage Images

Arcadia Publishing, the leading local history publisher in the United States, is committed to making history accessible and meaningful through publishing books that celebrate and preserve the heritage of America's people and places.

Find more books like this at
www.arcadiapublishing.com

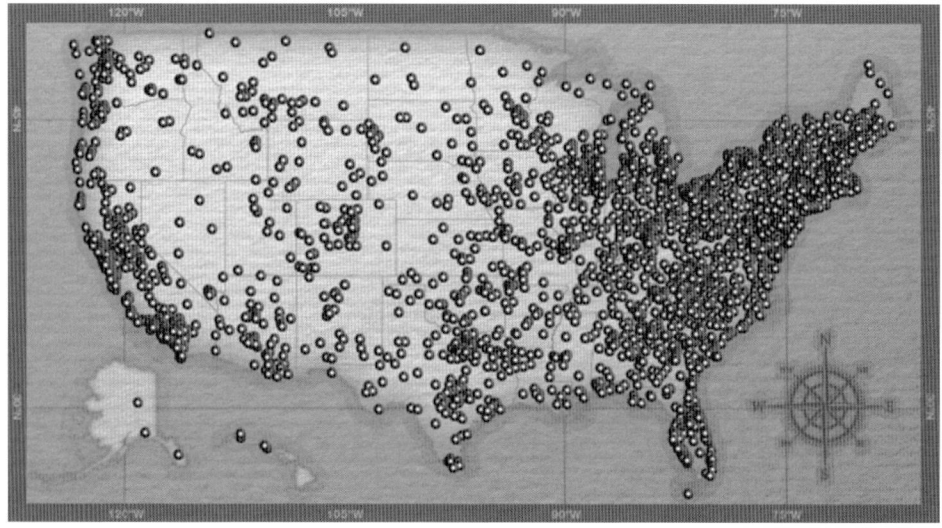

Search for your hometown history, your old stomping grounds, and even your favorite sports team.

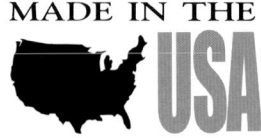